# POCKET PRECINCTS

# LISBON

A pocket guide to the city's best
cultural hangouts, shops, bars
and eateries

## DONNA WHEELER

*Hardie Grant*
TRAVEL

# CONTENT/

# INTRODUCTION

Astonishingly pretty, more often sunny than not, relaxed and egalitarian, culturally overflowing: no wonder Lisbon is the city on everyone's list. The Portuguese capital numbers only half a million people, but fills with close to five million visitors each year. Outside the well-worn tourist circuits, you can join the Lisboeta in living well: feasting on Atlantic seafood, listening to fado music or Afro–Portuguese electro, toasting sunset at a neighbourhood quiosque (outdoor bar), and heading to the beach for a swim or surf. It's intoxicating, whether you're here for a weekend or much longer.

Lisbon grew incredibly wealthy in the 16th-century on the spoils of Portugal's colonial empire, after Vasco da Gama's extraordinary voyages. Just enough of the seductively ostentatious Manueline architecture of this period survived the 1755 earthquake to remind you how wealthy it was, but it's the 18th-century sweeps of pastel daubed, tile-clad facades that give the city its character today. If these streetscapes occasionally feel lost in time, the city actually was for half of the 20th century under Salazar's 48-year dictatorship, but since 1974's Carnation Revolution Lisbon has blossomed into one of the world's most socially progressive cities.

Portugal was hit hard during the EU's 2008 debt crisis, but a spirit of reinvention has since seen a vibrant start-up sector, with the revival of traditional craft industries and abandoned spaces turned into all sorts of venues.

Lisbon has long been home to harmonious Brazilian, Mozambican, Angolan, Cabo Verdeanan and Macanese communities – this fertile mix forms the basis of the city's vibrant music scene. It's also why the city's culinary tastes roam far further than most of Europe.

Over-tourism has become a burden, yet Lisboeta remain some of the most welcoming people you'll ever meet. Search beyond the tourist trails and you'll be rewarded.

The city's gobsmacking good looks, its fleets of swooping swallows, its lust for life and its touching kindnesses will seem at odds with the Portuguese notion of saudade – the wistful presence of absence. It's only after you've left that Lisbon's intricate pull becomes evident: that's saudade for you.

**Donna Wheeler**

## A PERFECT LISBON DAY

My first Lisbon morning coffee is always at a local pastelarias, like **Aloma**, where I'll have a strong garoto (little latte) and a bolo de arroz (cupcake) for dunking. I'll go for a walk in the lush, magical **Jardim Botânico** or opt for some peace and contemplation in the **English Cemetery**. My second coffee is always at **Bettina & Niccolò Corallo**, not just because of their wonderful São Tomé chocolate but because it's the city's best coffee.

I'll next browse through one of my favourite shops in the world, **Casa Pau-Brasil** (you can never have too many glam Brazilian bikinis in Lisbon), and pop into their cafe for a salted chocolate brigadeiro for later on. A quick poke through the books downstairs at **Livraria da Travessa**, then onto lunch, which can't be hurried. I'll join friends at **Tascardoso** for grilled red mullet and a jug of vinho verde, or I might have a solo bitoque – steak, egg, chips and rice – and a little glass of Sagre at **Zé dos Cornos**. Then out to the **Museu Calouste Gulbenkian** to soak up the sun in the gardens and some quality time with the Persian ceramics and Flemish paintings. If it's a hot day, I might get an Uber to **Costa Caparica** (good thing I splurged on that bikini!) for a dip and a chat with the local surfers at **Dr. Bernard**.

Dinner will be a few interesting small plates at **Prado** and a glass of an excellent local wine. If tonight's going to be an early one, I'll go to **Damas** for a nightcap. Otherwise, I'll head to **The Bar** for a cocktail and some good company. It's nice to linger there, but it's time to head to **Água De Beber**, a musical pit-stop before **Titanic Sur Mer**. I'm there for the beautiful Rio Tejo (River Tagus) by night views, river breezes and whatever great live act happens to be on. Home, hopefully, by dawn.

# LISBON TOP ATTRACTIONS

# BEST FOR DRINKS

# BEST FOR CONTEMPORARY ART

# TOP LOCAL SHOPPING

# BEST FOR MUSIC

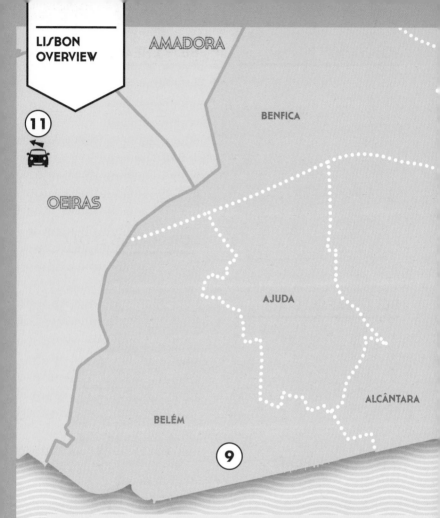

# LISBON OVERVIEW

AMADORA

BENFICA

(11)

OEIRAS

AJUDA

ALCÂNTARA

BELÉM

(9)

## PRECINCT/

x

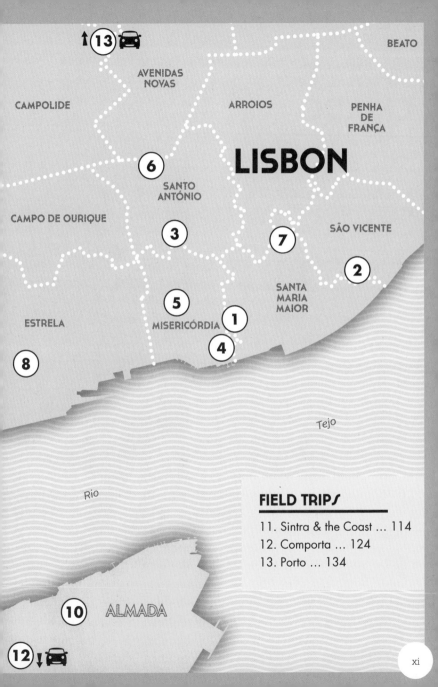

# LISBON

BEATO

AVENIDAS
NOVAS

CAMPOLIDE

ARROIOS

PENHA
DE
FRANÇA

(6)

SANTO
ANTÓNIO

CAMPO DE OURIQUE

(3)

(7)

SÃO VICENTE

(2)

(5)

SANTA
MARIA
MAIOR

ESTRELA

MISERICÓRDIA (1)

(4)

(8)

Tejo

Rio

(13)

(10) ALMADA

(12)

# BAIXA & CHIADO

The earthquake of 1755 and the subsequent tsunami devastated Lisbon's ancient heart, and today Baixa's grand, flat grid is an entirely 18th-century creation. Known as the Pombaline Downtown, from its architect the Marquês de Pombal, its formal mid-rise architecture and marvellous squares, like Praça do Comércio (*see* p. 2), give this part of the city pomp and rigueur. It remains one the world's most considered, planned centres (also, interestingly, one of the first to utilise earthquake-proofing building techniques). Cut through by the pedestrianised Rua Augusta, it's a true downtown, filled with businesses, restaurants and bars, including interesting new places like Prado (*see* p. 6), but also has its fairshare of traditional cafes, easygoing tascas (restaurants) and winebars that fill with local workers for lunch and after-work drinks.

Head west into bustling, but still occasionally bohemian, Chiado, for the city's most concentrated retail streets. Alongside global high street stores you'll find the world's oldest bookshop, Livraria Bertrand (*see* p. 3) and beachy local designers, such as Plus351 (*see* p. 5). Special but low-key places to eat and drink also cluster here, like A Taberna da Rua das Flores (*see* p. 7) and By The Wine (*see* p. 9). Up the hill from bustling Rua Garrett, there are trees and a couple of kickback quiosques (outdoor bars), in the square surrounding the Chafariz do Carmo fountain.

→ *Traditional architecture on the Largo Barão Quintela, Chiado*

# 1 PRAÇA DO COMÉRCIO

Arco da Rua Augusta, Baixa
Mon–Sun 9am–8pm
Metro Terreiro do Paço
[MAP p. 164 B3]

All boats sailing down the Rio Tejo (River Tagus) once docked by this magnificent square and the city's original gateway still impresses mightily on first sight. The high Pombaline-style on show represents the city's post-earthquake rebirth – the Ribeira Palace that occupied the site was destroyed by the tsunami in 1755 – but the square's three river-facing sides remain, daubed in a vivid yellow, and the triumphal arch **Arco da Rua Augusta** still stands at its centre. The equestrian figure in the centre on high is King Jose I. He overlooked the dramatic end to the Portuguese monarchy some years later, when Carlos I was assassinated by anarchists in 1908. You can take the lift to the top of the Arco da Rua Augusta for river views and city vistas or just wander the shady colonnades, visit cafes or do a wine tasting at **Viniportugal**. After dark, take in the nightly light projections that fill the entire square.

**POCKET TIP**
The Praça is home to Lisbon's oldest cafe, Martinho da Arcada. It has been serving coffee since 1782.

## 2 LIVRARIA BERTRAND

Rua Garrett 73-5, Chiado
Mon–Sun 9am–10pm
Metro Baixa-Chiado
[MAP p. 155 F2]

Thinking of this place as merely a shop would be missing the point. The books are mostly in Portuguese of course, though there is a limited English selection. But you come here to commune with fellow bibliophiles past and present: it's the world's oldest bookshop. From 1732 on (before the earthquake), Livraria Bertrand has drawn the country's intellectuals, as well as visiting writers and artists, philosophers, revolutionaries and conservatives. Founded by French booksellers Pedro Faure and Pierre Bertrand, the 'new' 1773 shop still has its original rambling rooms, stunning vaulted ceilings and dark wooden shelves. There are plenty of stacks to poke through, including a whole section dedicated to poet Ferdinand Pessoa in English translation. There are a small cafe at the very back if you need a quick reviving bica (espresso).

**POCKET TIP**

Raul Mesnier de Ponsard, a student of Gustave Eiffel, designed the extraordinary, if perpetually crowded, Elevador Santa Justa, that takes passengers from Baixa to Chiado's Largo do Carmo and the ruins of Carmo Convent.

3

## 3 BIRD ON A WIRE STUDIO

Largo Madalena 1, Baixa
Thurs–Sat 12pm–7pm
Metro Baixa-Chiado, bus 201
[MAP p. 164 C2]

Londoner Buki Fadipe combines East End cool and Lisboeta flair at this bright little shop, hidden up a short flight of stairs by the Igreja da Madalena church. It feels like walking into a stylish friend's airy apartment (a feeling helped along by a warm greeting from Buki's cute pooch). Vintage fashion finds are priced to please, as are a collection of sweet pumps and sandals, Rollas jeans, leather bucket bags, hoop earrings and gold plated-pendants inspired by ancient amulets. Homewares include ceramics and bright giclée prints. Everything comes from small, independent labels and local artisans.

**POCKET TIP**

You'll find the original A Vida Portuguesa (see p. 72) shop near Plus351 on Rua da Anchieta (no. 11), in a former perfume factory lined with dark wooden cabinets.

## 4 PLUS351

Rua da Anchieta 7, Chiado
Mon–Fri 10am–8pm, Sat–Sun 11am–8pm
Metro Baixa-Chiado
[MAP p. 155 F2]

Not so much surf wear as full coastal immersion, designer Ana Costa creates clothes that are comfortable, fluid and timeless. Everything is made locally and demonstrates the reputation for quality that the Portuguese textile industry has long been known for. While shapes are simple, and many pieces are unisex, there's a beautiful tactility that also makes them unique, say sweatshirt cotton used 'inside out', silky flamê cotton, linen or slubby jersey. Costa's usual palette of deep and vivid blues, sand, sunny yellow and moss green also evokes the wild places of the Portuguese coast and hinterland, making for truly local pieces. On a budget? Grab a stripey +351 tote (the label's name is a cute reference to Portugal's calling code) or head to the sales rack.

# 5 PRADO

Travessa das Pedras Negras 2,
Baixa
Wed–Sun 12pm–3.30pm &
7–11pm
Metro Baixa-Chiado, bus 201
[MAP p. 164 C2]

Roman remains aside, there's nothing timeworn or fusty about this former factory-turned-restaurant. Foliage tumbles from the lofty ceiling, industrial fittings hang above and there are soothing eau de Nil (pale green) walls and natural wood tables. The passion project of chef Antonio Galapito, Prado has filled a void in a city where there's little choice between casual tasca (traditional) tables and formal fine dining. Their locally grown ethos goes above and beyond, with dishes highlighting rare ingredients, specialist regional producers and traditional techniques. Hipsi cabbage, whey, black scabbardfish, Minhota beef and summer savoury are as poetic on the plate as they read. Natural wines are a little more expensive than the jugs of happy drink elsewhere, but are a chance to be guided through the country's most innovative and dedicated winemakers. Don't skip dessert: tangelo granita, panna cotta and beetroot or mushroom ice-cream with pearl barley, dulse and caramel will blow your mind.

**POCKET TIP**
Just around the corner from the restaurant, Prado Mercearia (Pedras Negras 35) has a groaning selection of take-home deli produce, as well as cakes and drinks done with signature Prado flair.

# 6 A TABERNA DA RUA DA∫ FLORE∫

Rua das Flores 103, Chiado
Mon–Sat 12pm–2.30pm &
5–11pm
Metro Baixa-Chiado
[MAP p. 155 D2]

It may not look like it from the outside (or from the inside for that matter) but this is one of the hottest tables in town. Rock up super early to put your name on the list, don't be surly about fellow tourists or a wait of an hour or two, and don't expect any coddling from the staff. Is it worth it? Indeed it is. Come at lunch for traditional dishes like the mythological-looking pescadinha de rabo na boca (tail in the mouth fish). At dinnertime the blackboard menu shapeshifts, with modern small plates that both respect and transform tavern staples. A tartare of local mackerel and green apple plays on the traditional picadinho de carapau (mackerel tartare), while iscas com elas (liver fried in pork fat) is rich but strewn with fresh herbs. Staff will take you through the chalked dishes, though you may need to press them for details beyond one or two 'favourites'. Wines, all from Lisbon and Tejo valley vineyards, are excellent – be happy to let the staff pour at will.

# 7 FÁBRICA COFFEE ROASTERS

Rua das Flores 63, Chiado
Mon–Sun 9am–6pm
Tram 24E
[MAP p. 155 D3]

Located in a quiet quarter of a steep little street, this industrial-looking cafe–roastery is a freelancers' favourite and an easy, laid-back place to get your mid-city bearings. Its narrow but cavernous bricked reaches are welcoming as the hubbub of roasting goes on at the back. Pour-overs are big here, but there are also special smooth blends used in the espresso and milk coffees. Summer treats include iced coffee, iced tea, cold brew chai and coffee lemonade. Brunch or lunch can be had with chicken or tuna salads, toasties and a neat range of brownies and pastries. If your Airbnb is lacking decent coffee equipment or supplies (it happens), here's the place to pick up an Aeropress and perfectly roasted and freshly ground single-origin beans.

**POCKET TIP**
Look out for Fábrica Coffee's bolthole (Rua das Portas de Sant Antão 136) in the posh Avienda Liberdade district, too.

## 8 BY THE WINE

Rua das Flores 41-43, Chiado
Mon 12pm–6pm, Tues–Sun
12pm–12am
[MAP p. 155 D3]

By all means be drawn here
for the pure spectacle of the
lofty vaulted ceiling lined with,
literally, thousands of top-to-
tail wine bottles. But there's
much more on offer that will
keep you propped up at the
bar long after you've paid your
respects to all that guzzled
vinho with a reverential
upwards gaze. José Maria da
Fonseca is Portugal's oldest
bottled table wine producer
(established 1834) and as
this is its flagship, tasting is
encouraged and there's a huge
range available by the glass.
Ask about their Alentejo DOCs,
reds made from indigenous
grapes, and produced in clay
amphora, known as talhas.
The house-baked Algarve loaf,
petiscos of octopus, cerviche,
cold partridge or roast beef
rolls, and fabulous Azeitão
cheese and Bellota sausage
boards are perfect pairings if
you're here for more than pre-
lunch or dinner tipples. This is
also an excellent place to pick
up a good quality bottle for
picnic or balcony drinking.

# 9 PALACIO CHIADO

Rua do Alecrim 70, Chiado
Sun–Thurs 12pm–12am, Fri–Sat
12pm–2am
Tram 24E
[MAP p. 155 E2]

Home in the 19th century
to the 1st Conde of Farrobo,
Joaquim Pedro de Quintela, the
very same noble whose name
became Portuguese vernacular
for 'party-hard', this palatial
pile has long known excess.
Today that mostly comes in
the way of decor – oh look,
there's a massive gilded lion
dangling from the ceiling!
But you can play at being
decadent by sipping artisan
gin at the **Junot Bar** (named
for the French general, whose
shameless luxury inspired
the expression: à grande e
à francesa, living large) or
popping the cork on another
bottle in the **Sabina's** room
under the brightly hued
frescos. If you do get a little
hungry, there are several
options, from charcuterie at
**Culatelo**, or seafood, cheese
platters and very prettily plated
tapas at **Barra**. Whatever
your mood, the view from the
second floor is worth the price
of a glass of wine (and the
occasional wait orchestrated
by the door mistress) alone.

**POCKET TIP**

It's super touristy but nothing can put a dampner on the historic beauty of Café A Brasileira (Rua Garrett 122); across the street is equally venerable manchester shop, Paris em Lisboa.

# ALFAMA & GRAÇA

Alfama's winding up-down-all-about paved streets and tangle of tiled residential buildings are one of the city's oldest areas, predating and surviving the 1755 earthquake, and built over Lisbon's Roman and Visigoth settlements. It's enchanting alright, but its main thoroughfares, like Rua dos Remédios, have become tourist trails that can zap it of much of its atmosphere. Strike out beyond those though and you can still discover squares and laneways that will make you sigh. Fado, Lisbon's melancholy folk music, has a strong presence here, home as it once was to generations of sailors and fishermen; head to Fado na Morgadinha (see p. 21) for a low-key but authentic fado experience. Lisbon's second major train station, Santa Apolónia, sits on the waterfront here, along with new shopping and eating-focused developments, and waterside clubs.

Further up the hill is Graça, a rapidly gentrifying neighbourhood that has thankfully held onto its quotidian heart, with a full complement of grocers, bakers and relaxed cafes, along with some new great wine bars and music venues, like Damas (see p. 20). Its views are, if it's actually possible, even more sublime than Alfama's. A bonus is its swathes of boldly political and hued street art.

→ Springtime jacaranda blossoms in Alfama

**SIGHTS**
1. Museu Nacional do Azulejo

**SHOPPING**
2. Benamôr 1925
3. Feira da Ladra

**EATING & DRINKING**
4. Agulha no Palheiro
5. Damas
6. Fado na Morgadinha

**DRINKING**
7. Bar Tejo
8. LuxFrágil

13

# 1 MUSEU NACIONAL DO AZULEJO

Rua da Madre de Deus 4,
Xabregas
Mon–Sat 10am–6pm
Bus 759, 794
[MAP p. 153 F2]

This is not just any tile museum, but Portugal's *national* tile museum and, apart from the exhaustive, exquisite collection of tiles, there's also its setting in the 16th-century **Madre de Deus** convent (itself also decorated to the hilt with tiles) to explore. While there are plenty of ancient examples, and an entire gallery of beautiful 20th-century and contemporary works, it's the period that charts the transition from Al-Andalus to high Baroque that's the most fascinating. The convent's chapel is also a stunning portrait of Portuguese Baroque overload, with its glade of carved wood and miles of celestial gilding. Don't miss azulejo panoramas, including the detailed, drone-like depiction of Lisbon before the 1755 earthquake, and the enigmatic, trippy scene known as *Singerie*: the Chicken's Wedding. Here a procession of monkey servants and lizard musicians accompany a lone chicken in a carriage. A casual **cafe** can be found in a delightful courtyard dripping in vines.

**POCKET TIP**
Got the fado music bug? Learn all about how Lisbon came to sing their very own blues at Alfama's Museu do Fado (Largo do Chafariz de Dentro 1).

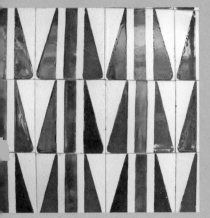

# 2 BENAMÔR 1925

Rua dos Baclhoeiros 20A,
Alfama
Mon–Sun 10am–8pm
[MAP p. 164 C3]

Situated in what's becoming
Alfama's most stylish square,
Campo das Cebolas, the
venerable beauty brand of
Benamôr has recently been
reborn and reimagined for
the 21st century. Some of the
original apothecary lines are
still made today, and a first
sniff and smear in this pretty
white tiled shop should be of
their near-mystical Créme de
Rosto and Alontoine. Then try
the new formulations, like the
rose-infused argan-oil-based
moisturisers (poetically named
Rose Amélie for the last queen
consort, Amélie of Orléans) and
Jacaranda, a scented tribute
to Lisbon's fleeting springtime
floral mascot. Packaging
is minimal, if luscious and
evocative, with Art Deco
shapes in black and a signature
tone for each line. Modern-
style products include bath
gels and a gorgeous scented
dry oil that gives the French
pharmacy equivalents a run for
their money. It's affordable too,
with handcreams and soaps
costing under €10.

# 3 FEIRA DA LADRA

Campo de Santa Clara, Alfama
Tues & Sat 9am–6pm
Metro Santa Apolónia, tram
28E, 12E
[MAP p.166 C1]

A Lisbon institution from
at least the 17th century,
this sprawling, chaotic flea
market – also known as the
Mercado de Santa Clara –
might be a tourist favourite
but has defied prettification.
There are professional-style
stalls selling cork bags and tile
fridge magnets a-plenty, but
there's also a huge number
of itinerant sellers who
spread their wares, spruiking
everything from old cassette
tapes to military uniforms, out
on a rug. Rummage for great
vintage clothes, as well as the
odd upmarket mid-century
design piece. This lofty part
of Alfama's far edge affords
beautiful views, as well as kind
breezes in the heat of summer.
Note that while the 'ladra' of
the title actually translates as
flea rather than thief, when
you're on the 28E tram, it's a
good idea to be mindful of your
wallet and phone.

**POCKET TIP**
Once you're done with
browsing the bric-a-brac,
there are a number of
cafes and bars around
Campo de Santa Clara
for a pitstop.

# 4 AGULHA NO PALHEIRO

Rua Jardim do Tabaco 5,
Alfama
21 090 7441
Wed–Sun 7pm–12am
Metro Santa Apolónia, tram
28E, 12E
[MAP p. 166 C4]

There are miles of places with signs declaring 'we have sardines' in Alfama's picturesque labyrinth, and you'll eat well, if not cheaply, at any of them. Here though, just a little down the hill near the waterfront, locals happily share the rustic tables in an old shopfront with visitors who've arrived by word-of-mouth or, by chance, stumbled past. Portuguese staples, including a tuna prego, cod with cabbage and potatoes, and, of course, sardines, are done in a fresh, simple style, with lovely accompaniments, such as Algarve carrots. Menu surprises include guacamole, tapandade and a perfectly done Fiorentine-style steak. If you're not already in a pastel de nata sugar overload, desserts are also interesting. Young, friendly staff are sweetly passionate about the menu. There are two sittings and it's best to call ahead to reserve. If you do need to wait for a table, they'll make you welcome with a beautiful glass of local wine or a well-made cocktail and a stool pulled up.

**POCKET TIP**

Ceia (Campo de Santa Clara 128), a sublimely simple 14-seater restaurant on Alfama's prettiest square, is Lisbon's most exciting, and exclusive, dining experience.

# 5 DAMAƧ

Rua da Voz do Operário 60,
Graça
www.vivalagenda.com/pt/p/
damalisboa or
www.residentadvisor.net
Tues–Thurs 1pm–2am, Fri–Sat
1pm–4am, Sun 5pm–12am
Metro Santa Apolónia,
tram 28E
[MAP p. 166 A1]

Exciting discoveries await at
Damas. The former industrial
bakery's warren of rooms all
have different moods, from the
sunny front spaces for coffee
during the day, to the kitchen-
side communal table for snacks
or dinner later on. Choose from
a meat, fish or vegan main
of the day, or a few dishes
from the petiscos (tapas-style)
menu. It's bold, eclectic stuff:
a bowl of chilli garlic prawns,
pica-pau veal with crunchy
pickled vegetables and
peixinhos da horta (tempura
green beans), or gazpacho and
a tranche of tuna with avocado
and tomatillas. The kitchen
staff's excellent taste in music
bodes well as the night wears
on. After dinner, you'll be ready
to head down the hall where
there's a band room/club and
different acts each night.
Check Damas' website for
upcoming gigs and note that
while most are free and there's
no door policy, on Fridays and
Saturdays they'll often reach
capacity around 2am.

**POCKET TIP**
The triangle of Largo da
Graça has some lively
little bars to hop between,
as does Tavessa do
Monte around the corner,
including the Venetian
import, Vino Vero.

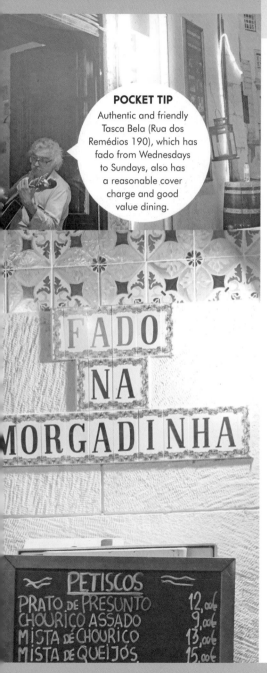

**POCKET TIP**

Authentic and friendly Tasca Bela (Rua dos Remédios 190), which has fado from Wednesdays to Sundays, also has a reasonable cover charge and good value dining.

## 6 FADO NA MORGADINHA

Largo Peneireiro 5, Alfama
Mon–Sun 12pm–4pm &
6.30pm–12am
Metro Santa Apolónia, tram 12E
[MAP p. 166 A4]

The mournful lyrics, resigned rubato and minor key guitar of fado music is the sound of Lisbon. The city is dotted with fado places, and Alfama has the greatest number of them, but it can be hard to find one that doesn't have a steep cover charge as well as pricey compulsory set-menu dining. Na Morgadinha is a low-key room on a pretty square, a little way off the main drag. It ticks all the fado boxes, with framed photos of the queen of song, Amália Rodrigues, and other fado greats, while its blackboard menu of tapas-style seafood plates, salads and pregos are reasonably priced and help assuage the cover charge. Once seated in the dimly lit room, you'll notice that this is fado vadio – the fado where anybody, and sometimes everyone, can join in with the songs of lost love, lives lost at sea and the hardness of it all.

# 7 BAR TEJO

Beco do Vigário, Alfama
Mon–Sun 10pm–2am
Metro Santa Apolónia
[MAP p. 166 B3]

Locals used to beg visiting travel writers not to blow the cover on this music-filled bar and, while it's no longer a close-guarded secret (the ensuing social media frenzy after an impromptu acoustic set from Madonna will do that), it's still a relatively under-the-radar treat. Knock on the door for admission. Once you're inside the well-patinated single room, there will *always* be something going on: the Brazilian owner, known as Mané do Café, may be playing his guitar or reciting poetry, his friends may be performing or you may just chance upon whichever famous musician is currently on tour, doing an impromptu after-midnight set. To keep the neighbours happy, everyone mimes clapping and otherwise keeps noise to a minimum. That said, there's a friendly vibe in the intimate space and even a little animated conversation in the surrounding courtyard. Wine, mojitos and beer are all reasonably priced.

**POCKET TIP**
Vinyl for sale and artisan beer are on offer at Do Vigário (Rua do Vigário 74), along with a small tasca (restaurant) menu and vegan snacks.

## 8 LUXFRÁGIL

Avenida Infante D. Henrique,
Armazém A, Cais da Pedra a
Sta Apolónia
Thurs–Sun 11pm–5am
Metro Santa Apolónia
[MAP p. 167 F2]

With two decades of service
to late-night fun, LuxFrágil
shows no signs of fading away.
Lisbon's party people still fill
its vast dance floor for house,
techno or disco nights. With
a little forward-planning, you
can catch a set or two from an
international name DJ most
weeks, especially if house is
your poison. Wallflowers can
take in the ever-changing
decor of the equally large
lounge bar on the second floor,
not to mention another small
dance floor. For those with the
stamina, there's nothing like
seeing the sun rise over the
Rio Tejo (River Tagus) from
the terrace on a midsummer's
morning. Doors may close
at 5am but the party often
continues until 9am, and
sometimes all day.

**POCKET TIP**

For amazing viewpoints,
head to the Miradouro
da Graça, with its lovely
church-side bar, and the
breathtaking, but by far the
busiest, Miradouro de Santa
Luzia, right above the
Alfama descent.

# PRÍNCIPE REAL & CAMPO DE OURIQUE

Not so long ago, Príncipe Real was considered a little too out of the way for visitors. Nowadays, it's often a destination in itself, with the continuous Rua Dom Pedro V and Rua da Escola Politècnica, and their many tributaries, packed cheek-by-jowl with smart cocktails bars, rowdy pubs, speakeasies and fashionable restaurants like A Cevicheria (see p. 30). Daytime wanderings reveal some of Lisbon's most interesting shops, including the sprawling, enthralling Casa Pau-Brasil (see p. 28) and Embaixada (see p. 29). This busy street has maintained its stately elegance though, as well as a hilltop airiness and beautifully vignetted views. At its heart is the Jardim do Príncipe Real (see pp. 26 & 31), where locals catch up under the spreading branches of the grand central Mexican cypress. For even more lush sprawling, the Jardim Botânico (see p. 26) tumbles down a hillside further to the north. Down the hill, where technically it's São Bento, you'll find antique shops, along with a small, tree-shaded square, the Jardim Fialho de Almeidath, surrounded by a calm clutch of bars and restaurants.

To the west, Campo de Ourique is still the upmarket suburb it has always been, if not a particularly sleepy one. A vibrant central grid of local shops and authentic places to eat like A Trempe (see p. 32) and Aloma (see p. 33) and the daily market make it a wonderful place to rent an apartment.

Tram: 24E, Metro Rato

→ *View across Campo de Ourique's Cemiterio dos Ingleses towards Príncipe Real*

**SIGHTS**
1. Jardim Botânico
2. Reservatório da Mãe d'Água das Amoreiras

**SHOPPING**
3. Casa Pau-Brasil
4. Embaixada

**EATING & DRINKING**
5. A Cevicheria
6. Tascardoso
7. A Trempe
8. Bettina & Niccolò Corallo

**DRINKING**
9. The Bar

# 1 JARDIM BOTÂNICO

Rua da Escola Politécnica 58,
Príncipe Real
Mon–Sun 9am–8pm (Apr–Oct),
Mon–Sun 9am–5pm (Nov–Mar)
Metro Rato, tram 24
[MAP p. 156 B1, 163 D4]

If you need any reminding of
Portugal's position on the very
edge of Europe, this botanical
garden is the place. An original
19th-century collection of
palms, cycads, succulents,
flowers, ferns and trees from
Portugal's former colonies
and trading partners mix with
even more subtropical exotica
from China, Japan, Australia
and New Zealand, including a
number of endangered species.
It's a lush oasis of winding
paths, enchanted groves
and viridian garden beds. Its
expansive proportions are not
immediately obvious – its four
hectares (10 acres) are entirely
hidden from the street – and
you really can lose all sense of
being in the city. Everything is
labelled, which will keep keen
gardeners and geographers
happy, or you can just walk,
laze and relax. If you're here in
spring, don't miss the dreamy
butterfly garden.

**POCKET TIP**
The snaking Mercado
Biológico (organic produce
market) sets up streetside
along the length of the
Jardim do Príncipe Real
each Friday and Saturday;
a perfect place to pick
up picnic supplies.

**POCKET TIP**

Delight in the gothic melancholy of historic Cemiterio dos Ingleses – the English Cemetery – in the delightfully overgrown grounds of historic St George's Anglican Church (Rua de São Jorge).

# 2 RESERVATÓRIO DA MÃE D'ÁGUA DAS AMOREIRAS

Praça das Amoreiras 10, Amoreiras
Tues–Sun 10am–12.30pm & 1.30–5.30pm
Metro Rato
[MAP p. 162 A3]

The 19-kilometre (11.8 mile) length of Lisbon's grand 18th-century aqueduct leads to this strange and ephemeral museum. Oh-so off the tourist trail, the one time reservatório (reservoir) and temple to the city's water supply is a beautiful example of architectural form *not* following function. An approximately five-million-litre pool gently laps beneath an array of water-themed sculptural follies, along with some fascinating relics of 19th-century industrial design. Stairs lead up to a rooftop that affords astonishingly high views of the city rooftops and river, as well as the aqueduct itself, stretching off into the distance. Downstairs, the echoey, dappled chamber is a cool respite on a scorching summer's day. Cultural exhibitions, including art shows, are a bonus.

# 3 CASA PAU-BRASIL

Rua da Escola Politécnica 42,
Príncipe Real
Mon–Sat 10am–10pm, Sun
10am–8pm
Metro Rato, tram 24
[MAP p. 156 A1]

This stunningly renovated 18th-century palace is a voyage of discovery for anyone not familiar with Brazilian design, or an exciting reacquaintance for those that are, with over 18 brands to browse. **Phebo**'s jewel-toned glycerine soaps in their vivid, nostalgic packaging and beautifully packaged single-origin chocolates get the senses acclimatised. Resort-wear from **Melissa** jelly bean sandals to beaded hi-shine bikinis from **Água De Coco** evoke Bahia days, while dramatic party wear from high-end designers like **Juliana Herc** are decidedly urban. The seductive, organic forms of Brazilian Modernism can be found in a rambling design showroom, along with new furniture by the exuberant **Campana Brothers**. Take a coffee break at the **cafe** and sample brigadeiros – Brazil's condensed milk flavour bombs. Downstairs, design-oriented bookshop, **Livraria da Travessa**, is a browsing delight.

**POCKET TIP**

Running down into São Bento from Rua da Escola Politècnica, the steep length of Rua de São Bento has many of the city's best vintage and antique dealers.

## 4 EMBAIXADA

Praça do Príncipe Real 26,
Príncipe Real
Mon–Sat 12pm–8pm, Sun
11am–7pm
Metro Rato, tram 24
[MAP p. 156 B2]

Portuguese designers and
makers are showcased here in
one of the Príncipe Real's grand
palacetas (small palace), in a
fabulous neo-Moorish wedding
cake of a building. There are
**Ecolã's** earthy luxe Burrel wool
capes, jumpers and blankets
from the high country of Serra
da Estrela, as well as the
relaxed Atlantic beachwear of
**Latitid**. Portugal has long been
known for its finely crafted
children's wear and is one of
the last places in Europe where
there's still a thriving textiles
industry – beautiful pieces for
babies and kids up to 12 years
can be found at **D.O.T**. There
are also homewares, ceramics
and organic skincare to pore
over, but the two floors –
lined as they are with murals
of magnificent nudes and
heavenly clouds – are worth a
wander even if you aren't
a shopper.

### POCKET TIP

For a night on the tiles,
literally, head to the Embaixada
atrium bar Gin Lovers, or for
a slap-up steak dinner to the
rambling basement of Atalho
Real below, where the cuts
are global but the wines
are Portuguese.

PRÍNCIPE REAL & CAMPO
DE OURIQUE

## 5 A CEVICHERIA

Rua Dom Pedro V 129,
Príncipe Real
Mon–Sun 12pm–12am
Metro Rato, tram 24
[MAP p. 156 C2]

Fish, grilled or fried, is a
Portuguese staple but venture
under the tentacles of A
Cevicheria's dangling octopus
for an entirely different seafood
paradigm. Local celeb chef
Kiko takes Peru's favourite
dish ceviche and, using the
best local fish he can find,
creates a seasonal menu that
draws not only from South
America but also Asia and
the South Pacific. There's a
vibrant, child-like glee to each
dishes' plating, with spheres
of tapioca balls and quinoa
making magical landscapes,
and foams added to glistening
white cubes of fish at the table.
There are tacos, empanados
and Peruvian causas, seafood
and potato dishes, if you don't
feel like raw. Even if you can't
snare a table (it's first come,
first seated, both around the
huge bar or at one of the tables
in the sparsely decorated
space), you can still be part of
the action. The pisco window
welcomes those who wait or
those who are just here for
pre-dinner drinks: grab a pisco
sour or a beer and join the
happy footpath-parked crowds
(it can be even *more* fun than
being inside).

**POCKET TIP**
Book ahead for Local's
(Rua de O Século 204)
innovative degustation dinner
(there's only ten communal
seats), or queue for upmarket
traditional dining at
Tapisco (Rua Dom
Pedro V 80).

30

# 6 TASCARDOSO

Rua de O Século 242,
Príncipe Real
Mon–Sat 12pm–3pm &
7–11.30pm
Metro Rato, tram 24
[MAP p. 156 B2]

Lisbon is dotted with tascas
(traditional restaurants) that
draw lunchtime crowds for
Portuguese comfort food and
a beer. This cosy two-storeyed
place opposite the Jardim do
Príncipe Real is no exception
to the norm, and at lunchtime
it fills with office workers,
local creatives and retired
folk. It's more subdued, if no
less crowded, at night, when it
draws more of a visitor crowd.
Steak and egg with rice and
potatoes might be your tasca
go-to, and while Tascardoso's
take on it is good, it would be
a shame not to work your way
through its excellent seafood
menu or try some of its more
unusual meat offerings, like
slow-cooked pork cheeks or
stewed rabbit. Ask your waiter
for the local catches of fish or
if the açorda (a super typical
prawn and bread soup with a
risotto-like texture) is on … if
it is, try it.

## POCKET TIP

Hang with the locals at
Jardim do Príncipe Real's
cafe or twin quiosques
(outdoor bars), while on the
last Saturday of the month
there are bric-a-brac
market stalls.

# 7 A TREMPE

Rua Coelho da Rocha 11,
Campo de Ourique
Mon–Sat 12pm–3pm & 7–10pm
Metro Rato, tram 24
[MAP p. 160 B2]

This is Portuguese soul food, earthy and bold, a sweet place that draws lunching locals in numbers or has a more relaxed date night vibe at night. Both the decor and the menu are a homage to the Alentejo, the central and coastal regions to Lisbon's south. At night, there's a long menu of both meat and seafood dishes to navigate (an I'll-have-what-she's-having stance can prove fruitful). Or during the day, there's a no-stress two-option dish for lunch for €13. The choice might be between a huge ceramic platter piled with bacalhau à bras – shredded salted cod with green olives and parsley – or an equally huge ceramic platter of Portuguese surf 'n turf, such as carne de porco à Alentejana, a pork and clam braise with paprika. Vinho da casa comes in half or full jugs.

**POCKET TIP**
Campo de Ourique's big name restaurant draw is Tasca da Esquina, a polished, upmarket take on traditional dining by chef Jose Avillez.

## 8 BETTINA &
## NICCOLÒ CORALLO

Rua da Escola Politécnica 4,
Príncipe Real
Mon–Sat 10am–8pm
Metro Rato, tram 24
[MAP p. 156 A1]

You'll know you're close to
this little cafe well before
you see it – the come-hither
scent of coffee and chocolate
pervade the street. House-
roasted beans here range from
around the world, but if you're
keen to keep things 'local',
opt for a single-origin from
former Portuguese colony São
Tomé and Príncipe. The other
starring beans – cocoa – are
also sourced from a family run
and sustainable plantation on
the dual island nation. You may
be content with the wafer of
complimentary chocolate that
comes with each coffee, or you
can choose from one of the
dark but delicately flavoured
barks: try sesame or the gutsier
Algarve flor de sal and caramel.
Other things to tempt are:
brownies, scrolls, a beyond-
moist chocolate cake and, in
summer, chocolate sorbet, or in
winter, hot chocolate. If you're
not already sold, yes, this *is* the
best coffee on the strip (made
on a shiny lime La Marzocco,
with spring water, no less).

**POCKET TIP**
For pastel de nata
perfection without the
crowds, head to pretty and
calm Aloma (Rua Francisco
Metrass 67) in Campo
de Ourique for morning
coffee and pastry.

# 9 THE BAR

Travessa Monte do Carmo 1,
Príncipe Real
Tues–Thurs 7pm–12am, Fri–Sat
7pm–2am
Tram 24E
[MAP p. 156 A2]

Beyond the evening crowds,
as the streets fall back down to
the centre, this simply named
and simply imagined concrete
box corner bar is a local's
local. Australian expat Teresa
Ruiz, the local behind the bar,
makes some of the city's best
cocktails, often joining guests
on one of the high wooden
stools for a chat. Early in the
evening, grab a bench under
the Tamara Alves mural for a
Sagre, a perfectly made G&T
garnished with juniper berries
and rosemary, or something
from the negroni menu (the
Cynar variety comes highly
recommended). Nibble on the
endlessly replenished popcorn,
be lolled by the happiness-
inducing indie soundtrack and
find yourself here late in the
little room filled with a friendly
mix of neighbours, expats
and the occasional traveller.
It's a special place: from the
minute you walk through the
door, you'll be welcomed like
you're one of the crew.

**POCKET TIP**
Picturesque Mercado de
Campo de Ourique is
a Time Out Market (see
p. 39) in miniature, open
daily 10am–11pm, with
places to eat-in, alongside
a daily neighbourhood
produce market.

**POCKET TIP**

Speakeasies dot this precinct: bar crawl your way between Asian-style Pavilhão Chinês (Rua Dom Pedro V 89), jazz-age Bar Procópio (Alto de São Francisco 21) and Art Nouveau Foxtrot (Travessa Santa Teresa 28).

# BAIRRO ALTO & CAIS DO SODRÉ

There's plenty of nightlife in all corners of the city but it's these two neighbourhoods that have given Lisbon its party-hard reputation. Walk down the pretty, pedestrianised grid of Bairro Alto (up-district) mid-afternoon, and you'd be hard pressed to see why, as while its historic, human-scaled streets are gorgeous to wander, beyond Rua de São Pedro de Alcântara, most of the shutters will be drawn. It's a different matter twelve hours on, when all streets west of Rua São Pedro de Alcântara's main thoroughfare – such as Rua do Norte, Rua da Atalaia and Rua do Diário de Noticias – are packed solid with plastic cup-swilling crowds.

South across Rua de São Paulo, where the steps are ever steeper, Cais do Sodré is Lisbon's old red-light district, and here the revelry continues. Beneath the Rua do Alecrim overpass it's impossible to miss the heaving Rua Nova do Carvalho, now universally known as Pink Street, or Rua Cor-de-Rosa, where you'll find natural wine bars alongside clubs in former strip clubs and, well, a few remaining strip clubs. Just before you hit the waterfront, Time Out Market (*see p. 39*) fills an entire block and its many restaurant stalls will have you agonising over food and wine choices morning, noon and night. By day, the extravagantly tiled, but still workaday, Rua São Paulo has surprisingly peaceful places to grab a coffee, including the pretty, vaulted freelance den, Comoba (*see p. 41*).

→ *Original pharmacy azulejos (tiles) at Comoba café, Cais do Sodré*

# 1 IGREJA & MUSEU DE SÃO ROQUE

Largo Trindade Coelho,
Bairro Alto
mais.scml.pt/museu-saoroque/
Mon–Sun 9.30am–5pm
Tram 51E
[MAP p. 157 E4]

As the saying goes, it's always the quiet ones you have to watch: the austere exterior of this mid-16th-century Jesuit church really gives no clue as to what's inside. Its several chapels and four altars are lushly embellished with gilt, marble, alabaster and all manner of semi-precious stones in a range of styles from the Mannerist ceiling to a couple of further centuries of Baroque and beyond bling additions. Catholics have an advantage here, as by far the best way to bathe in the extraordinary atmosphere is by attending Mass (times vary). Stillness will grant you time for the trompe-l'oeil above to reveal its many layers. Tours in English happen daily – check the website for details. There is an attached museum with even more ecclesiastical loot on show. The church is just by the stunning Miradouro de São Pedro de Alcântara.

**POCKET TIP**

An old convent at the Museu Nacional de Arte Contemporânea do Chiado (MNAC, Rua Serpa Pinto) is filled with 19th- and 20th-century Portuguese art.

# 2 TIME OUT MARKET

Avenida 24 de Julho 49, Cais do Sodré
www.timeoutmarket.com/lisbon/en
Mon–Sun 10am–12am
[MAP p. 154 C4, 169 F1]

The city's venerable Mercado Ribeira was transformed in 2014, into what must be one of the world's largest food halls, care of Time Out. Communal tables fill the centre of the vast space and turn over hundreds of diners each day. What it lacks in intimacy, it more than makes up for in conviviality and choice. This book could devote an entire chapter to its numerous counters alone – there are 26 of them at last count, as well as shops, a huge club and live music venue, and some of the original market traders who still ply fresh produce and flowers. Each of the counters has been 'curated' or specially chosen by *Time Out* reviewers as the best of the city, whether that's the juiciest prego (Portuguese steak sandwich), the most flavoursome bacalhau (salt cod), the freshest sushi, the sweetest seafood and so on. All of the city's celeb chefs are represented: it's a great first stop when new to town to get your culinary bearings. See the market's website for a calendar of cooking classes, and listings of concerts and events.

# 3 VALDO GATTI PIZZA BIO

Rua do Gremio Lusitano 13,
Bairro Alto
www.valdogatti.com
Mon–Sun 12pm–11pm
[MAP p. 157 D4]

Lisboeta are as fond of Italian food as the rest of us, and there's no shortage of pizza to be had across the city. Valdo Gatti stands out for many good reasons, the most compelling is their dough. Authentic as all get out, it's made with 100 per cent Italian organic wholewheat flour, a natural yeast mother, olive oil and sea salt. That's it. All toppings are organic too, and there are some simple but not-so-ordinary choices, like the summer favourite Crudaiola Antonino, with raw cherry tomato, rocket, mozzarella and parmesan. Cooler nights call for the Tuscan sausage, pancetta, potato and rosemary pizza or a roam across to the small pasta menu for an excellent eggplant parmigiana or lasagna. The pretty, plant-filled vaulted dining room is small so book online for a before-7pm table or take a drink on the footpath and wait. Take-away and delivery are also possible.

## 4 COMOBA

Rua de São Paulo 99, Cais do
Sodré
Mon–Sun 7.30am–7.30pm
Metro Cais do Sodré
[MAP p. 154 B3]

This is not your usual corner
cafe to down a quick
pingado and a pastel de
nata (Portuguese custard
tart). Instead, join expats
and laptop-wielding local
freelancers and settle in at
this large and gorgeously tiled
spot. Oat milk, almond milk?
No problem. Matcha latte?
Of course. Vegan gluten-free
pancakes or a vurger (that's
a vegan burger)? Absolutely.
The healthy, sensitive menu
at Comoba's is refreshing in
this city and the fresh, organic
brunch and lunch dishes come
beautifully plated, strewn with
flowers or greens. Health goals
aside, they also do a mean
Bloody Mary, a beautiful freshly
squeezed Mimosa and a green
apple breakfast gin juice. And
yes, the coffee is flawless.

## 5 ZÉ DOS BOIS & 49 DA ZDB

Rua da Barroca 49 & 59,
Bairro Alto
Wed–Thurs 10pm–2am, Sat &
Sun 10pm–3am
Metro Baixa-Chiado
[MAP p. 155 D1]

Right in the heart of the Bairro Alto mayhem there is a little haven of cool spread across two buildings. Cultural association Galeria Zé dos Bois hosts a rambling upstairs bar, bookshop and exhibitions at number 59, while downstairs 49 Da Zdb is part bar, part venue with late DJs and, on some nights, experimental music concerts. Upstairs is like wandering into a house party, complete with vintage furniture, beers stashed in a fridge and cheap drinks in plastic cups – all kinds of fun and with a low-key, low-lit terrace from which to chat and peer at the throngs below. Downstairs offers a wider selection of drinks, and past the packed dance floor, there's a calm courtyard. Both levels are super LGBTQIA+ friendly. The discreet entrances to both bars mean they also escape the worst of the street's excesses. The **bookshop** has a huge range of contemporary art, literature and humanities titles and Portuguese artist books published by ZdB; come early to explore the bookshop and exhibitions from 6pm.

**POCKET TIP**
*The* fado music place in Bairro Alto, poster-lined Tasca do Chico (Rua do Diário de Notícias 39) is permanently packed and, if you're not averse to other visitors, always fun.

**POCKET TIP**

A cocktail favourite, Pensão Amor's (Rua do Alecrim 19) splendidly decadent interior tilts to its former incarnation as a house of ill repute.

# 6 O BOM O MAU E O VILÃO

Rua do Alecrim 21, Cais do Sodré
Sun–Thurs 7pm–2am, Fri–Sat 7pm–3am
Metro Cais do Sodré
[MAP p. 155 D4]

Looking for a rowdy, raucous night out but not quite the debauch of Pink Street or Bairro Alto? Serious clubbers may turn up their noses at the party tunes, but in a city where electronica, house and techno dominate, the O Bom DJ's penchant for disco classics and dirty funk can feel like a holiday in itself. There's seemingly another hidden bar or potted palm enclave to discover every visit and if you're here before midnight, there is a calendar of film events and concerts. Earlier in the evening, it's an easygoing choice for pre-bar hop shots and a sprawl on one of the many sofas.

# 7 ÁGUA DE BEBER

Travessa São Paulo 8, Cais
do Sodre
Tues 7pm–2am, Wed–Sun
7pm–4am
Metro Cais do Sodré
[MAP p. 154 C4]

This old mariners' drinking
hole is nestled between the
Cais do Sodré bar strip and
the Time Out Market (see
p. 39) bustle, and named for
the Antônio Carlos Jobim
song popularised by Astrid
Gilberto. The caipirinhas are
cheap, the sangria is strong,
there's a pie-warmer full of
tasty coxinha (chicken patties)
and the shoulder-to-shoulder
regulars are unfailingly friendly.
An afternoon drink under the
sailor's knots is sweet, but this
is, in fact, the place to come
to hear MPB (música popular
brasileira). Sunday nights
are music nights (others are
too but not with certainty),
when musicians set up in the
tiny bar and the crowd spills
out into the night, happily
taking over the surrounding
pedestrianised street.

**POCKET TIP**
A civilised, if never, ever
dull, addition to Cais do
Sodré's Rua do Corpo
Santo scene, is smart little
wine bar Bacchanal at
no. 28.

**POCKET TIP**

B.Leza next door (Cais da Ribeira Nova) has an equally eclectic weekly line-up of live music, including the incredible Angolan Kizumba dance nights on Sundays.

# 8 TITANIC ſUR MER

Cais da Ribeira Nova,
Armazém B
Thurs–Sun 11pm–6am (other
nights for scheduled acts)
[MAP p. 169 F1]

The Titanic feels like the dockside warehouse it once was, complete with close up Rio Tejo (River Tagus) views from its back doors and where river pebbles replace an actual terrace. It's all about the night, though: acts range from gypsy punk to techno to something endearingly known as Beyoncé fest. Look out for the regular Monday jazz jam, with improvisation from local jazz students and visiting musicians. And if you're lucky enough to be in Lisbon on a Sunday, don't miss what's billed as Europe's most authentic rodas de Samba (an Afro–Brazilian 'wheel' performance, where musicians play in a tight circle). A line-up of ridiculously talented Brazilian musicians and singers draw a crowd and the dancing goes until 4am, check their Facebook page for details. Mojitos and beer are reasonably priced and there's minimal fuss at the door.

# SANTA CATARINA, BICA & SÃO BENTO

Elevated Santa Catarina is a fashionable, fluid zone, with spectacular views, not least from Miradouro de Santa Catarina (*see* p. 48). It sits between the heavy (foot) traffic of Chiado and Cais do Sodré, and seamlessly flows into soulful São Bento and then riverside Santos beyond. Rua do Poço dos Negros has long been a commercial thoroughfare but after a period of decline late last century, again throngs with city life. Third-wave cafes almost outnumber old-style places like Zapata (*see* p. 54) around here. There are artist-run projects and shops like Mini Mall (*see* p. 50) and Boutik (*see* p. 52) to explore, too, while bars and clubs such as Park (*see* p. 56) and Incógnito (*see* p. 57) tend to hide themselves away.

Fabulously historic Bica stretches down the hill from mid-city Calçada do Combro. It's another of the city's ancient pre-earthquake neighbourhoods, full of cobbled streets, painted houses, little fountain-graced plazas (Bica, in fact, means water fountain), and possibly Lisbon's most photographed street: Rua da Bica de Duarte Belo. There's also some of the most dizzying up and down stretches that those Lisbon hills can come up with; thighs suffer but all eyes are on the beautiful Rio Tejo (River Tagus) views.

→ *Ascensor da Bica, the Rua da Bica de Duarte Belo funicular railway*

**SIGHTS**
1. Miradouro de Santa Catarina
2. Ascensor da Bica

**SHOPPING**
3. Mini Mall

**SHOPPING & EATING**
4. Boutik

**EATING**
5. Manteigaria
6. Zapata

**DRINKING**
7. Park
8. Incógnito

# 1 MIRADOURO DE ʃANTA CATARINA

Rua de Santa Catarina S/N,
Santa Catarina
[MAP p. 154 B3]

If you only have time for one
miradouro – the city's beloved
lookouts – make it this one.
There's a full sweep of Rio Tejo
(River Tagus) to take in, all the
way to the Ponte 25 de Abril
(25 April Bridge, see p. 106)
and beyond to the Cristo Rei
(see p. 106). It's spectacular, if
perhaps not as spectacular as,
say, the Miradouro da Graça or
Miradouro de Santa Luzia (see
p. 23). But this miradouro is not
*entirely* about the view. First
there's the strange statue of
Adamastor that watches over
all – a mythical sea monster
from the epic Portuguese poem
*The Lusiads*. Then there's the
quiosque (outdoor bar), serving
your standard wine, porto and
beer; it's one of the city's best
situated and most lively, along
with impromptu live music.
*Ver navios do alto de Santa
Catarina* (literally, seeing ships
from the top of Santa Catarina)
is now Portuguese idiom but
still rings true – this is a great
place just to hang out.

**POCKET TIP**
Just above the Miradouro
is the curious Museu da
Farmácia, which documents
5000 years of pharmacy.
It has an attendant
health-themed restaurant;
its terrace is a choice
sundowner spot.

## 2 AΓCENΓOR DA BICA

Rua da Bica de Duarte Belo,
Bica
Mon–Sun 7am–9pm
Metro Cais do Sodré, tram 25E,
28E
[MAP p. 154 C1]

Tram-spotters and tourists
line up for one of the world's
cutest public transport rides.
The ascensor (also known as
the elevador) might be styled
in yellow just like the 28E
tram but is in fact a funicular,
or funicular-like railway. It
performs an elegantly up–down
route along the Rua da Bica de
Duarte Belo, between the Rua
de São Paulo with Calçada do
Combro/Rua do Loreto (you
can board at either end). The
tiny cars always run together,
as counterweight for each
other's ascent and descent.
It's a fun, if brief, ride but if
there are queues, the hip flexor
testing descent down the
narrow footpaths on each side
of the rails affords similar Tejo
views. Walking also gives you
the opportunity to break your
journey with a coffee or beer
at one of the many bars (*see*
pocket tip) lining the route.

**POCKET TIP**
Bars line Rua da Bica
de Duarte Belo's length;
try Petiscaria do Elevador
for mojitos and caipirinhas
made with real Brazilian
love, or cheap wine,
poetry and jazz tunes
at Lua da Bika.

# 3 MINI MALL

Rua Poiais de São Bento 120A,
São Bento
Mon–Sat 11am–8pm
Bus 714, tram 28E
[MAP p. 159 E2]

With the express aim to represent designers and makers that you won't find along luxury strips the world over, the whitewashed and light-flooded Mini Mall has the city's best fashion offering and is a beautiful encapsulation of true Lisboan style. Incredible party wear from cult labels like Sunad from Marid, Korea's Muséd and InDress from Paris, sit beside bargain vintage pieces; the common element is the stylist owner's great eye. There are also cabinets of traditional Portuguese jewellery, shelves groaning with folky Bordallo Pinheiro ceramics, and one-off leather shoes and bags. A true, if petite, concept store, there's also local olive oil, sunglasses and socks, and upstairs, there's a collection of vibrant Berber rugs and beach-ready raffia bags. Staff are as in love with everything on display, as you soon will be too. Even browsing here feels like hanging out with new friends.

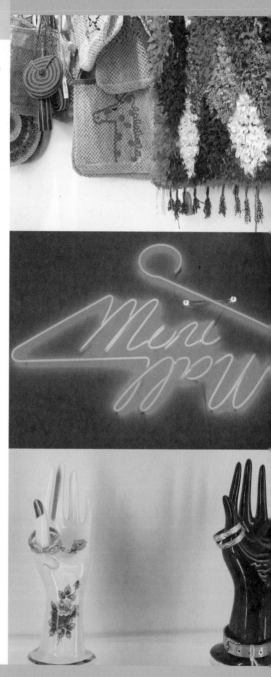

**POCKET TIP**

French accents abound throughout Lisbon but dominate in the patisseries, wine shops and bistros of Rua de São Bento, Lisbon's Little Left Bank.

# 4 BOUTIK

Rua de São Bento 106D,
São Bento
Mon–Sat 9am–7pm, Sun
9am–6pm
[MAP p. 159 E1, 161 F4]

Surf's up at Lisbon's very
own surf shack every day of
the week (and, yes, there are
waves, under a 30-minute
drive away). A space totally
dedicated to the coastal life,
you can pick up a board
(to buy or rent), board wax,
organic sunblock or Australian-
made TCSS boardshorts
here, and browse the best
of Portugal's surf, skate and
streetwear brands. Pat the
friendly house labrador on your
way through and then linger on
in the **cafe**. Choose between
the poké bowls (diced raw fish)
named for legendary surf spots,
including Portugal's own
Nazaré, or there's Japanese
tataki, avocado on toast, a
huge choice of smoothie
bowls and carb-loading
pancake stacks.

# 5 MANTEIGARIA

Rua do Loreto 2, Santa Catarina
Mon–Sun 8am–12am
[MAP p. 155 D2]

Bite into a pastel de nata
(Portuguese custard tart) and
you'll notice that butter plays, if
not a starring role, a big part in
its success or failure. This tart-
only bakery fittingly occupies a
former butter factory and takes
its name from its predecessor.
The pastel de nata here have
their dedicated fans – if you're
fond of cinnamon, you'll
soon be one, too – but the
overwhelming appeal is the
open kitchen. Watch bakers'
every move as they plough
butter into flour, knead and
stretch the pastry and pour
in the custard. Then see the
tarts emerge from the oven and
onto your plate still deliciously
warm. Yes, it's fine to specify
the level of burnish, and yes,
the coffee's good too.

# 6 ZAPATA

Rua do Poço dos Negros 47,
São Bento
Wed–Mon 10am–4pm &
6.30pm–12am
[MAP p. 159 F2]

This tiled cervejaria (seafood-focused beerhall) has an old-timers, aka smokers, front bar and a couple of rooms of tightly packed tables where you'll most likely end up. The mildly frantic atmosphere and bare-bones decor don't equate to bargain prices, however you can under order and still be absolutely overfed. This is some of the city's best seafood, simply and expertly prepared, and if you've been hankering for grilled sardines, this is one of the best non-waterfront places for them. But also look to the scrawled handwritten specials, where you may find daily catches like percebes, goose barnacles, or burrié, sea snails, and non-aquatic icons like the rich boiled meat dish cozido and pica-pau – a fried pork stew.

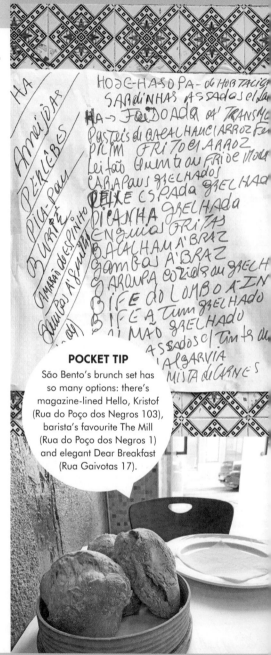

**POCKET TIP**
São Bento's brunch set has so many options: there's magazine-lined Hello, Kristof (Rua do Poço dos Negros 103), barista's favourite The Mill (Rua do Poço dos Negros 1) and elegant Dear Breakfast (Rua Gaivotas 17).

# 7 PARK

Calcada do Combro 58,
Santa Catarina
Mon–Sun 1pm–2am
[MAP p. 154 A1]

A rooftop bar with a super
obscure location if ever there
was one (it's perched on top
of a graffiti-strewn carpark,
seven flights up), don't be
surprised at how popular Park
is. In peak spring into summer
sunset season, you'll need to
forego any notion that you're
not part of a traveller and expat
pack. But it's worth it for the
well-made cocktails and the
burgers, as well as *that* view,
which takes in all of Lisbon and
the charming church rooftop
right next door. Plus, the leafy
clubhouse vibe is endearing, as
are the smiling staff. Note that
after midnight, long after the
view-greedy have gone hard
and gone home, DJs begin and
the vibe shifts into something
far more interesting.

## 8 INCÓGNITO

Rua dos Poiais de São Bento 37,
São Bento
Wed–Sat 11pm–4am
Metro Baixa-Chiado, tram 28E
[MAP p. 159 F2]

Google maps will send you the wrong way and the actual street address delivers you to a blank door. Yes, it's called Incógnito for a reason. Late (like really late) on weekends though, navigation skills will not be necessary as you'll spot the crowds and possibly also sense that club bass thump in your bones. Once you've found it, ring the doorbell for admittance. Ancient in club years at 30, Incógnito is the city's indie queen, with a classic disco interior, a bijou dance floor and lots of electropop and new wave tunes. Earlier in the week, make sure to come after midnight, as nothing will be going on before then except a few keen young party-goers smoking at the bar.

# LIBERDADE

Avenida da Liberdade is more than an avenida (avenue). Long a byword for luxury, this grand, tree-lined strip is where you'll find most of the city's posh hotels, posher shops (think Cartier, Miu Miu, Louis Vuitton and Gucci concessions), embassies and modern multinational offices (and, in charmingly, disarmingly Portuguese fashion, the Lisbon HQ of the PCP, that is, the Portuguese Communist Party). The last decade has seen both the avenida itself and its surrounding neighbourhood streets get their groove back, with a new batch of far more interesting upmarket options, from the sprawling luxury juggernaut JNcQUOI (see p. 67) to easy-going Delidelux (see p. 62) and Sky Bar (see p. 66). The avenida remains a grand, leafy and unusually broad place to stroll in an otherwise steep and winding city, with Art Nouveau architecture and decorative motifs that will also grab your attention (see p. 61).

Shopping may seem like the focus on the avenida but this is also the city's place for celebration and protest. On Dia da Liberdade each 25 April, carnation-carrying Lisboeta gather here to commemorate the Carnation Revolution, the coup that overthrew the Salazar dictatorship and gave birth to the new democratic Portugal, while in June it's the focus for the city's famed Santo António celebrations (see p. 150).

At the avenida's northern end, beyond the Marquês de Pombal roundabout, the grassy expanses and clipped hedges of Parque Eduardo VII (see p. 61) make up Lisbon's largest inner city park. A little further north of here is the wonderful Museu Calouste Gulbenkian (see p. 60) and its equally impressive gardens.

→ *Traditional tilework along Avenida da Liberdade*

# 1 MUSEU CALOUSTE GULBENKIAN

Avenida de Berna 45A,
Avenidas Novas
Wed–Mon 10am–6pm
Metro São Sebastião, Praça
de Espanha
[MAP p. 173 B1]

Housed in what was the first Modernist building to be classified as a national monument in Portugal, there are over a thousand works on show at this richly endowed private art museum, considered one of the best private collections in the world. Petroleum baron and astute collector Calouste Sarkis Gulbenkian amassed more than six thousand paintings, sculptures, ceramics and books from antiquity to the early 20th century, from both Europe and the Middle East. The purpose-built Founders Collection includes a wonderful room of Flemish masters, haunting Florentine portraits, Houdon's marble *Diana* and standout works by Gainsborough, Turner, Manet, Degas and Monet. Gulbenkian also had a particular eye for the decorative arts: there's exceptional glass work by René Lalique's glass, masterpiece rugs from Persia and Turkey, and Bibles and bowls from Armenia.

**POCKET TIP**
The Gulbenkian's two 1960s buildings are pristinely preserved, even down to the pure, functional design of the cafeteria. They were designed in conjunction with the deeply verdant, surrounding gardens.

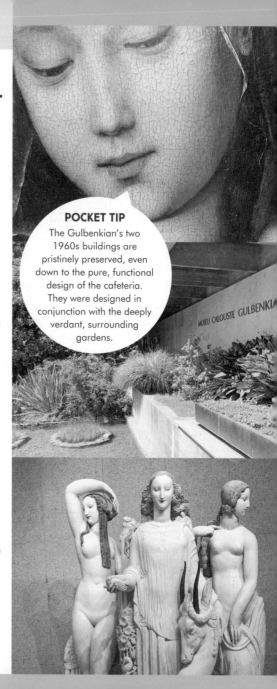

**POCKET TIP**

The formal garden and promenade of Parque Eduardo has sweeping views of the city and river, lots of lolling space and two early 20th-century estufas (greenhouses), full of tropical flora to visit.

## 2 AVENIDA DA LIBERDADE ARCHITECTURE

Metro Avenida
[MAP p. 163 F4]

If you're suddenly sensing Paris déjà vu as you stroll this grand avenida (avenue), there's nothing uncanny going on. The Passeio Público, a post-earthquake 18th-century gated park built for local nobility, was transformed in the 1880s into the grand boulevard you see today, complete with Champs Elysee-style avenues shaded by plane trees. A number of the avenida's original ornate 19th-century and Art Nouveau buildings have survived, although they are now mostly international hotels. The great swathes of patterned cobblestone footpaths called calçadas also date back to its 19th-century glory days. This Portuguese town planning feature really does get star billing on the avenida, with abstract and floral designs reaching all the way from Praça dos Restauradores up to Praça do Marqués de Pombal. Look for painter João Abel Manta's designs at **Restauradores**.

61

# 3 DELIDELUX

Rua Alexandre Herculano 15A
Sun–Thurs 10am–10pm, Fri–Sat
10am–11pm
Metro Avenida
[MAP p. 163 D2]

**POCKET TIP**

Fine-dining hotspots in
Liberdade include the
pretty Eleven (in the Jardim
Amália Rodrigues) and
the imaginative pan-
Med Open Brasserie
Mediterrânica (Rua de
Santa Marta 48).

For a food obsessed city,
Lisbon has a dearth of high-
end food emporiums, but
Delidelux – cafe, grocery store
and delicatessen – changed
all that. Pick up all manner
of beautifully packaged
food products to take home,
including the ever-ubiquitous
tinned fish but also wonderful
local olive oils, chocolates
and biscuits. Supermarkets in
Portugal can often disappoint,
but here you can create a
perfect picnic with beautiful
Azores fruit, rustic sausages,
the best of presunto (cured
ham), foie gras and small-
producer Azeitão or Serra da
Estrela cheese. The former
industrial building has had
a smart, contemporary fit-
out and has great terrace
tables that work whether
you're here for early fruit and
pastries, weekend brunch,
comforting toasties and salads
at lunchtime, or a petiscos
(Portuguese tapas) spread
later. These dishes utilise
what's on offer in the deli,
from Portuguese favourites
like tuna pica-pau (sliced with
pickles) to Italian burrata and
carpaccio, and French terrine.
There's another branch handy
to Santa Apolónia station.

**POCKET TIP**

If you're a designer devotee or just up for a spot of high-glam window shopping, pop into Fashion Clinic (Tivoli Fórum, Avenida da Liberdade 180) for Paula Amorim's astute European label edit.

# 4 JE*U* É GOÊS

Rua São José 23, Liberdade
Mon–Sun 12pm–3pm, 7–11pm
Metro Avenida
[MAP p. 157 F1]

Ganesha greets you here first
sporting a crown of thorns,
and then so does Jesus Lee,
chef, owner and chief pourer
of Super Bocks. He arrived in
Lisbon from his hometown of
Goa as a teenager and after
cooking in some of Lisbon's
busiest kitchens, this is his
first restaurant. From its
extraordinary mural, peopled
by Hindu gods and Catholic
saints, to an ultra-intriguing
menu, it's certainly a departure
from the usual. The Portuguese
have been connoisseurs of
curry since the colonial-era
expeditions of Vasco da Gama
(in fact, vindaloo is a telling
portmanteau of the Portuguese
'vindalho', wine and garlic).
Jesus has made his name with
thoughtful interpretations
of classic Goan dishes, each
telling a story of centuries of
influence and synthesis, of
colonial and local fusion.
Shrimp samosas come with
an intensely green herb paste,
there's traditional shrimp
curry with ladyfingers, crab
with coconut and eleven-spice
goat. Or try the fascinatingly
earthy spiced mushrooms
and chestnuts, and one of the
daily specials, where Jesus
gets creative.

**POCKET TIP**
Lisbon is dotted with
Goan diners, some
still going strong since
opening in the '60s,
just after Goa gained
independence from
Portugal.

## 5 AſſOCIAÇÃO CABOVERDEANA

Rua Duque de Palmela 2,
Liberdade
Mon–Fri 1–6pm
Metro Marquês de Pombal
[MAP p. 163 D1]

You could be under the
impression that you're on your
way to Accounts Payable in
the lift of this workaday office
block, but it has a secret.
Cabo Verde – another of
Portugal's colonies that won
independence in the 1970s –
might be a four-hour flight
south of the equator, but here
on the eighth floor it feels very
close indeed. The island's
cultural organisation has a
lunchtime dining room where
expats, friends and the culinary
curious gather. The menu
changes daily, but along with
the curries or tuna steaks, the
cachupa, the island's national
dish, will *always* be on. A
rough-cut, bay-scented soupy
stew of corn, beans, cassava
and sweet potato comes with
either pork, fish, chicken or
goat. Kriolu will often be the
language of those around
you, and on Tuesdays and
Thursdays, there will be music
and dancing, as essential
to Cabo Verdeana identity
as cachupa.

# 6 SKY BAR

Hotel Tivoli, Avenida da
Liberdade 185
Mon–Sun 5pm–1am
Metro Avenida
[MAP p. 163 E3]

On top of the Hotel Tivoli, Sky
Bar is one of the most relaxed
of Lisbon's more upmarket
rooftop bars and, a bonus, it's
open all year-round. Sunset
cocktails come with the
expected panoramic views,
with a startling perspective
on the avenida (avenue), its
swathe of green running to
downtown and then the Rio
Tejo (River Tagus) beyond.
There's a nicely topological
layout to explore, plenty of
comfortable, cushion-strewn
corners to commandeer, or
high bar stools for maximising
views. Both the bar and snack
menu are overseen by the
hotel's fine dining restaurant,
**Seen**. Cocktails like the
Spritz Moniz, a redolent fizz
of white port, vinho verde,
cinnamon, anise and orange,
or a spearmint spiked Pisco
Sour are fun without being
gimmicky. Pair them with a
few orders of fish tacos, sushi
and lamb croquettes, and call
that dinner. Before you know it,
if it's the weekend, the DJ will
have arrived. Note: children
under 12 are not permitted,
and no thongs, aka flip-
flops, allowed.

**POCKET TIP**

The biggest night on
Avenida Liberdade is the
Marchas Populares, held on
the feast of Santo António,
on 12 June, when a singing,
dancing troupe from each
city neighbourhood
performs.

**POCKET TIP**
Venture down into the basement of JNcQUOI for the velvet hush of the Assouline bookstore and pore over the coveted travel and lifestyle titles.

# 7 JNCQUOI

Avenida da Liberdade 182-184
Mon–Wed 10am–12am,
Thurs–Sat 10am–2am, Sun
12pm–12am
Metro Avenida
[MAP p. 163 F3]

While this building's days as an historic theatre are long gone, luxury hub JNcQUOI (pronounced as the French je ne sais quoi) conjures a similar realm of fantasy and drama. There are three dining spaces here, all of which welcome those just in for an early evening drink or a quick daytime refreshment. The forest tones, leather, marble and glossy white woodwork in the upstairs restaurant are achingly stylish, but still can't compete with a huge, if not lifesize, T-Rex skeleton hovering over the space. Downstairs there are the casual cosy bar stools of the **DeliBar** and for warm weather, the interior garden and tropical vibe of **Terrace at JNcQUOI Asia**. This is not somewhere to pop into for the usual cheap vinho verde, with one of the city's best cellars and a remarkable collection of wine, including rare Madeiras, 'out of the box' Portuguese red and whites, and top bottlings from around the world. Late nights can also be fun: yes, that's a DJ booth in the unisex toilets.

# MOURARIA, MARTIM MONIZ & INTENDENTE

If you like your neighbourhoods with a little grit, and a lot of life, Mouraria is your kind of Lisbon. The 12th-century Arab quarter – hence the name – escaped major 1755 earthquake destruction so still has the feel and flavour of the tightly knotted medieval city. There's noticeable gentrification, but it's mostly added even more to explore in an already complex mix. Hidden squares filled with locals taking the air, bolthole bars serving nothing but ginja and beer, and the lilt of fado music's sad chords on the air are still the norm. Up above it all is the hugely atmospheric Castelo de São Jorge (*see* p. 70).

Praça Martim Moniz is the city's main multicultural hub; a new crop of bars have now joined its cheap Asian, Indian and African restaurants and shops. The action continues to move north, taking in much of the original neighbourhood of Arroios. Largo do Intendente is one of the city's grandest and prettiest squares but for years was run down and verging on a no-go zone. Not so now. Remodelled in 2012, but still without a hint of twee, it's lined with lively bars, large and small, as well as some beautiful shops like A Vida Portuguesa (*see* p. 72). It's also rumoured that this is where Soho House will open its Lisbon location.

→ *Typical architecture of Largo do Intendente*

**SIGHTS**
1. Castelo de São Jorge
2. Tram 28E

**SHOPPING**
3. A Vida Portuguesa

**EATING**
4. Cervejaria Ramiro
5. Chinês Clandestino
6. Cantinho do Aziz

**DRINKING**
7. Topo
8. Casa Independente

# 1 CASTELO DE SÃO JORGE

Rua de Santa Cruz do Castelo, Castelo
Mon–Sun 9am–9pm (Mar–Oct), Mon–Sun 9am–6pm (Nov–Feb)
Bus 737, tram 28E
[MAP p. 165 B4]

Lisbon's long history has a palpable presence on every street corner, but it's while wandering the ramparts of the city's 11th-century castle you really do sense a millennia and more of this city's past. The strategic hilltop settlement has seen the Phoenicians, Romans, Visigoths, Arabs and French come and go. A highlight, apart from some utterly captivating views from the extant ramparts, is the archeological site. Access is via hourly free tours – your erudite guide will tell you vivid tales of daily life in a home from the Al Andalus period of the 11th-century, as well as show you the remains of a 7th-century BC Phoenician kitchen. There are also a few ceramic treasures in the small **museum**. A couple of sweet courtyard **cafes** provide refreshments under the shade of ancient pine trees. And yes, that's the resident peacock you heard honking in the distance.

## POCKET TIP

Sadly there's no public bar in Palacio Belmonte, Lisbon's most beautiful hotel that sits just below the Castelo de São Jorge, in the atmospheric Pátio de Dom Fradique. But dine at stylish French restaurant Grenache here, instead.

**POCKET TIP**

Worth a wander for
20th-century architecture
devotees are the residential
backstreets of Anjos
and Alameda, lined
with apartment buildings
built in high Art
Deco style.

## 2 TRAM 28E

Praça Martim Moniz, Martim
Moniz
[MAP p. 165 A3]

Yellow on the outside,
wood-panelled on the inside,
Lisbon's endearing vintage
trams are an unexpected
tourist phenomena. Eléctrico
28's winding route from gritty
inner city Martim Moniz to
toney, leafy Campo de Ourique
takes in some of the city's
most spectacular hilltop vistas
and beguiling narrow streets.
Somewhat a victim of its own
undeniable appeal, its queues
and crowds have made it an
unviable form of transport for
locals. If you're keen and want
a seat, be prepared to wait for
over an hour at the originating
stop in Martim Moniz, or head
up to Prazeres or Praça São
João Bosco in Estrela and take
the tram back down (you can
also hop on at any of the stops
along the way, although you'll
have to squeeze on, stand and
be mindful of pickpockets).
Alternatives? Walking the
route is fun. Or the quick Baixa
circuit of 12E works nicely if
you're just longing for the tram
experience itself. Otherwise,
the 24E's ascent from Largo
do Camões in Chiado to
Campolide gives you some
hill thrills, too.

71

# 3 A VIDA PORTUGUE/A

Largo do Intendente Pina
Manique 23, Intendente
Mon–Sun 10.30am–7.30pm
Metro Intendente
[MAP p. 165 B1]

For its Portuguese customers, everything in this superstore holds a nostalgic appeal. For visitors, it's an enticing, inspiring place to buy locally made presents and keepsakes. Owner Catarina Portas has collected or commissioned a huge range of iconic Portuguese items, from affordable, easy-to-pack items like Couto toothpaste and handcream, Viarco children's pencils in gorgeous original boxes, biscuits and sardines, to artisan pieces like intricate filigree jewellery from Travassos in the north, and traditional cotton bedspreads and rugs from the south. If you've been enchanted by the nightly flight of the city's swallow population, grace your home with your own andorinha, a touching re-edition from the original moulds of master ceramist Rafael Borgalo Pinheiro. This store, in the old Viúva Lamego tile factory, has over 6000 items in stock, including a huge range of homewares and a dedicated **children's bookshop**.

**POCKET TIP**
The Arquivo Fotográfico de Lisboa (Rua Palma 246), a public photography archive, has lovely temporary exhibitions on its ground floor.

# 4 CERVEJARIA RAMIRO

Avenida Almirante Reis,1-H,
Intendente
Mon–Sun 12pm–12.30am
Metro Intendente
[MAP p.165 B1]

Catch word of the queues, its busy road location and a vibe-killing entry ticket system and you might be tempted to skip Ramiro. Rest assured though, Ramiro has been serving up what is truly the city's best seafood since 1956. It's set in a delightfully intact cantine-style interior, with a vivid under-the-sea tile mural and gurgling fish tanks of what will soon be on your plate. Choose from a staggeringly large menu and soon plates of razor clams, clams in garlic, tiger prawns, goose barnacles or lobster will appear one or two at a time, preceded by a stack of toasted bread rolls. Keep to a budget by choosing less extravagant items or less of them, or go with it and drop €50 for a splendid three-hour feast. The tipple of choice here is beer: there's a good selection or do what the Lisboeta do and order an uma imperial (20cl) of Sagres. Locals know that late afternoons are the best time to snag a table. Ironically for such a seafood star, it is also famous for its prego (steak sandwich).

**POCKET TIP**

Cultural centre and cult venue Anjos 70 (Regueirão Anjos 70) runs a nightly bar, occasional club nights and, once a month, hosts a massive weekend vintage and makers' market.

# 5 CHINÊS CLANDESTINO

Rua da Guia 9, Mouraria
Mon–Sun 6.30pm–12am
Metro Martim Moniz
[MAP p. 165 B3]

To be entirely clear, this is not the actual name of the restaurant but of the phenomena – pop-up Chinese restaurants with a semi-legal status – to which the restaurant belongs. But this restaurant (which doesn't have a name, beyond its street address) is the easiest of the Chinês Clandestino to find and one of the longest running. Feeling like somewhere that might morph into a dance party 'round 3am, the space is raw and strip-lit. The menu is huge and you're handed a pad to write down the numbers of the dishes you want. It's very easy to over-order – dishes are cheap and serves are comically large, including the complimentary prawn crackers. Rounds of ravioli frito (pork dumplings) are what everyone around you will be doing for starters. Mains run from familiar, westernised standards to authentic Macaense and ultra-spicy southern Chinese dishes, including some tasty vegetarian options like chilli tofu and eggplant.

**POCKET TIP**

You can find under-the-radar clandestinos in apartment kitchens and living rooms by scanning the upper windows of Mouraria's little streets, like Rua do Benformoso, Rua da Guia and Rua do Capelão. Look for the jauntily hung Chinese lanterns.

# 6 CANTINHO DO AZIZ

Rua de São Lourenço 5,
Mouraria
Mon–Sun 9am–11pm
Metro Martim Moniz
[MAP p. 165 B4]

The colonial-era relationship between Mozambique and Portugal was as troubled as it was long, but one legacy is the city's Mozambican presence today, which is a greatly enriching one. Up in one of Mouraria's ancient hilltop alleys, this family-run cantinho has been serving Mozambican specialties since not long after independence – some thirty years. It's a place of warm welcome, cold beer, culinary spice and brilliant east African tunes. Fried yuca is the signature entrée, while lamb chacuti (a rich coconut stew) or curried goat are must tries, as is the peanut-enriched makoufe, a crab and prawn curry that's served with coconut rice. Curry-starved palates will welcome the hit of heat and complex seasoning of most dishes (the influence of southern Indian cooking is clear, as, in turn, is the Mozambican in both the Portuguese and Brazilian kitchen). The terrace tables are a treat on a sunny day or on warm nights.

**POCKET TIP**

The São Jorge-bound escalator can help with the walk up to Cantinho do Aziz from Martim Moniz if your legs protest the steps.

# 7 TOPO

Centro Comercial Martim
Moniz 6 Esq, Praça Martim
Moniz, Martim Moniz
Sun–Thurs 12pm–12am, Fri–Sat
12.30pm–2am
Metro Martim Moniz
[MAP p. 165 A2]

Lisbon is a city of memorable
rooftop bars, but for a change
from those that populate the air
space of its glammest hotels,
Topo offers a new view and
a little more soul. Despite its
quasi-secretive location (it sits
on top of a six-level shopping
mall full of import–export
clutter, but is well signed if you
look up) and hectic surrounds,
it's far from grungy inside.
A young, friendly and local
crew crowd the large outdoor
terrace and there's also a vast
glass-fronted restaurant space
with an extended central bar. If
the scene outside is too amped
or the music not to your taste
(there's a DJ most nights),
pull up a bar stool inside.
Snack on moreish Brazilian,
Mexican and Asian-fusion bar
food and order classic cocktails
or house specialties like the
sloe gin-based Roxanne or the
frothy rum-based Pineapple
Express. And that view? City
hills tumble in all directions,
São Jorge sits before you and
the Topo sign glows red after
sunset's done its brilliant
nightly fade.

**POCKET TIP**
Throw back plastic
cups of ginja – Portugal's
cherry flavoured fire
water – at down and
dirty bar Os Amigos
da Severa in the
Mouraria maze.

## 8 CASA INDEPENDENTE

Largo do Intendente Pina
Manique 45, Intendente
Tues–Thurs 5pm–12am, Fri–Sat
5pm–2am
Metro Intendente
[MAP p. 165 B1]

Casa Independente was where the true Intendente precinct renaissance began and the fun continues. Climbing the stairs and following the sound of happy regulars down the hall, it can feel as if you've stumbled into an endearingly shabby chic share house. There's a great blackboard wine list, all available by the glass or the bottle, and lots of small easy things to eat, from spicy croquettes to sweet pastries. Once that's sorted, there's an intriguing warren of rooms to explore, art shows to take in and, finally, a sofa to linger on. Night or day, the real gem though is its large courtyard with fairy lights and dangling vines. And later, the **Tiger Room**, a dancefloor-slash-band venue kicks off, with anything from Belgian electro DJs to local psych rock bands or Brazilian funk, given the night.

**POCKET TIP**
Other Largo do Intendente bars: cosy Secadegas at one end, bubbly Josephine at the other and in between, excellent wine at Bordalo II in the Hotel 1908.

# SANTOS, LAPA & LX

Stretching west towards Belém is Santos-o-Velho, or simply Santos, a once working class precinct of tiled apartment buildings and riverside warehouses. The galleries, cafes and artisan shops moved in a decade ago, but its traditional life still lingers and it has retained a strong sense of community and neighbourhood rhythms, while also knowing how to party.

Lapa is its upmarket sibling up the hill, where genteel streets are dotted with low-key places to eat. Further west again is Alcântara, an old Arabic name meaning 'the bridge'. That bridge today is modern Lisbon's enduring symbol, the Ponte 25 de Abril (25 April Bridge, see p. 106), a soaring piece of 1970s architecture and named for the revolution that came a few years after its opening. LX Factory (see p. 84) has transformed this industrial neighbourhood and is one of the world's most successful and vibrant repurposings of an old industrial site. Its sprawling network of retail, cafes and bars are a day-to-night playground for visitors and locals alike.

→ *The colourful streets of Santos*

**SIGHTS**
1. Museu Nacional de Arte Antiga (MNAA)
2. Museu da Marioneta

**SHOPPING**
3. LX Factory
4. OBG (obrigado. obrigada)

**EATING & DRINKING**
5. Le Chat
6. Senhor Uva
7. Heim
8. Rio Maravilha

# 1 MUƒEU NACIONAL DE ARTE ANTIGA (MNAA)

Rua das Janelas Verdes, Lapa
Tues–Sun 10am–6pm
Metro Santos, bus 714
[MAP p. 169 D1]

This grand yellow pile holds Portugal's most important collection of painting, sculpture and decorative arts from the 11th century on. It is however a refreshingly laid-back experience, with a good chance you'll get many of its key works to yourself for a good, unhurried gaze. Nuno Gonçalves' *Painéis de São Vicente* (*Panels of St Vincent*) is a breathtaking work of narrative naturalism; and you must see the *Belém Monstrance*, a highly decorated gold ecclesiastical vessel from 1506, made by poet Gil Vicente with East African tribute gold given to Vasco da Gama during his second voyage. There are also works by European masters such as Lucas Cranach the Elder, Piero della Francesca and Albrecht Dürer. Don't miss the fascinating, and often highly symbolic, pieces brought back from Portugal's colonies long ago, including a serene Virgin and Child which references Bodhisattva Guanyin and was fashioned from Mozambican elephant ivory in one of Macau's territories.

## 2 MUƧEU DA MARIONETA

Rua da Esperança 146,
Madragoa
Tues–Sun 10am–6pm
Metro Santos, bus 714
[MAP p. 158 C4]

If the nearby Museu Nacional de Arte Antiga (MNAA, *see* p. 82) is ridiculously sublime, this puppet museum is all about the sublimely ridiculous. Rooms are dimly lit and its huge cast of puppets are spotlit against black-backed cabinets, conjuring the feeling of an actual performance. There are beautiful pieces from around the world, including exquisite wayang kulit and golek from Indonesia, but it is the Portuguese collection that is the most fascinating. These tell stories about the varied folk traditions of the country, as well as puppets from the era of the Salazar dictatorship that were used to disseminate political ideas during the heavy censorship of those years. There are also excellent temporary shows and the pretty courtyard of the former convent is used for concerts.

**POCKET TIP**
Dine in a walled garden at the Clube de Jornalistas (Rua das Trinas 129), a Modern Portuguese restaurant in a rambling old private club.

# 3 LX FACTORY

Rua Rodrigues de Faria 103,
Alcântara
Bus 201, 714, 760
[MAP p. 168 B1]

A sprawling post-industrial
site nestled under the Ponte
25 de Abril (25 April Bridge,
*see* p. 106) in Alcântara, is now
a vibrant mini-city. LX Factory
has kept the far from glossy
atmosphere of the former
textile factory and printers but
filled the space with colour
and round-the-clock life. Mid-
morning the cafes fill with
creatives popping down from
their studios on the factory's
upper floors, while on weekend
nights, it's a boozy street-
art daubed indoor–outdoor
funpark. Shopping highlights
include the vast bibliophiles
delight, **Ler Devagar**, with
excellent Portuguese–Asian
restaurant **Malaca Too**. There
is also a wine shop, **More
Than Wine**. Great cafes
abound, but for excellent
(chocolate) cake, head to
**Landau Chocolate**. Hungry?
There's wood-fired fare and
a cute vintage atmosphere
at both **1300 Taberna** and
**Cantina LX**, tasty tex-
mex **Mez Cais** and simple,
free-range Portuguese-style
chicken in smart surrounds
at **Cucurico**. Brazillian bar
**Rio Maravilha** (*see* p. 91) is
perched on a rooftop here.

**POCKET TIP**
LX Factory hosts a
huge vintage and
makers' market,
every Sunday
11am–7pm.

# 4 OBG (OBRIGADO. OBRIGADA)

Rua das Janelas Verdes 90, Madragoa
Mon–Sat 11am–7pm
Metro Santos, bus 714
[MAP p. 169 D1]

Two Santos locals have filled their sunny shop with a wonderful range that captures the Lisboetan lifestyle: easygoing, earthy and stylish. Here you'll find t-shirts, clogs and plimsoles, bags and homewares – all organised by colour, and all of which recall the many shades of the Portuguese landscape. You might be drawn to the hand-turned ceramics from which you could equip a whole kitchen. If you're shoe-inclined, you will be excited by the affordable, wearable styles with chunky boots, pointy flats and fuzzy Birkenstocks in winter and platform espadrille slides and cotton loafers in summer. Plain t-shirts – colour-coded of course – are another strong point. If you've got a little one to dress, you might even luck upon a faux sheepskin set of dungarees, or look out for their chunky cotton cardigans in moody blacks and greys.

## 5 LE CHAT

Jardim 9 de Abril, Lapa
Mon–Sun 12.30pm–2am
Metro Santos, bus 714
[MAP p. 169 D1]

Unless you happen to be idling in the park after a Museo Nacional de Arte Antiga (*see* p. 82) visit, Le Chat is easy to miss. Ironic, given it takes the spectacular form of an elongated glass box, hovering over a cliff. Its position and expanses of glass, along with a full-length terrace make for wonderful river and bridge views, including some ever-compelling dockside vignettes. With the knockout view, the paintings on the wall seem superfluous, but there's much else to love about the streamlined contemporary interior. Weekend brunches are served until 5.30pm or join ladies who lunch and local business people for big, healthy salads and tuna or steak pregos, or just coffee, during the week. At night, the tonal theatre of sunset and the sparkle of lights makes it a romantic spot for a cocktail or wine, a snacky dinner – or stay late for DJs and more drinking.

**POCKET TIP**

Bakery Gleba (Rua ior do Crato 14) uses old Portuguese grain varieties in its much ught-after sourdough ead; try their broa de ho, a cornbread from Northern Portugal.

# 6 SENHOR UVA

Rua Santo Amaro 66A, Lapa
Wed–Thurs 5–11pm, Fri–Sun
3–11pm
[MAP p. 161 D3]

Just down the hill into Lapa from the peaceful green of Jardim da Estrela, Stephanie and Marc, two young expats from Montreal, have reinvented the corner wine bar. Walls are whitewashed, table tops are marble and there are piles of cushions on banquettes to nestle into. All the wines are natural and the list features Portugal's most innovative producers, alongside some very interesting European bottles; Marc will take you on a tasting tour across the continent. Glasses filled, Stephanie creates a daily changing menu of innovative, beautifully presented vegetarian sharing plates, like spring asparagus with crispy red kale, walnut milk, leeks and lima beans or cauliflower cake with chives, spicy mayo and slaw. Even the details are delightful: cult westside baker Gleba (see p. 87) delivers the bread and it's served with sheep's milk butter.

**POCKET TIP**

In summer, grab a picnic to-go from Senhor Uva and join local families at the glorious Jardim da Estrela.

# 7 HEIM

Rua Santos-O-Velho 2,
Madragoa
Wed–Mon 9am–7pm
Metro Santos, bus 714
[MAP p. 158 C4]

This sunny corner is where
Santos merges into Madragoa,
though the friendly neighbourly
vibes continue along the length
of this cafe, grocer and bar-
lined street. Brunch in the sun
at Heim, either by the window
or at one of the coveted
footpath tables – a favoured
Sunday pastime for locals.
Full fry-ups are one way to go,
or there's avocado on toast,
fruit-strewn pancake stacks,
quinoa patties or granola. The
coffee is excellent and there
are freshly pressed juices
and smoothies, including the
vitamin bomb of red berries,
bananas, micro greens and
almond milk. Lemonade gets
its own menu section, and it's
hard to pass up the spider-
like lemonade and ice-cream.
During the week it's a little less
packed but young freelancers
fill the tables most mornings
and afternoons. Fresh flowers
all around must make it feel
as if it's a treat to come to
work here.

**POCKET TIP**
So popular for its
brunches, gluten-free
and vegan menu and
excellent coffee, there are
queues each weekend
at Cherie Paloma
(Calçada Marquês
Abrantes 148).

**POCKET TIP**

Young Lisboeta often gather for pre-club refreshments at the clutch of bold brassy bars lining Largo Santos.

## 8 RIO MARAVILHA

4th floor (entrance 3)
LX Factory, Rua Rodrigues de Faria 103, Alcântara
Tues–Thurs 12.30pm–2am, Fri–Sat 12.30pm–3am, Sun 12.30pm–12am
Bus 201, 714, 760
[MAP p. 168 B1]

If you think you've exhausted your Lisbon rooftop quota, think again. LX Factory's (see p. 84) most spectacular bar – found up a few flights of non-descript stairs – combines cutting-edge architecture with a beautifully eclectic interior. There's a huge internal bar, an almost equally expansive terrace, an upmarket-leaning restaurant and all manner of nooks and crannies to explore or hide away in, many of them sharing the river and bridge views of the outside spaces. The friendly Brazilian bar staff keep the cocktails flowing – the classics are done well with lots of fresh citrus and herbs – but the house specials are surprising and complex, such as Smoky Passion's tequila mezcal one, two hit with the fruit punch of passionfruit, pineapple and coconut, or a whiskey sour with peanut and caramel. Snacks take their lead from the excellent Brazilian–Modern Portuguese fusion of the restaurant.

# BELÉM & CASCAIS

Historic Belém, to the west of Lisbon, was once a separate riverside city, its shipyards and docks the launching place of Portugal's Age of Discovery in the 15th century. The Rio Tejo (River Tagus) grows wide here, the Atlantic breezes seem saltier and the pace slows a little. Torre de Belém (see p. 94), a late Gothic limestone tower, guards the riverfront, a shimmering historic counterpoint to Belém's other landmark, the Padrão dos Descobrimentos (see p. 95). Today Belém trades on its cultural clout, with both the MAAT (see p. 98) and Museu Coleção Berardo (see p. 95) being just two of its museums. It's also home to the glorious 500-year-old monastery, Mosteiro dos Jerónimos (see p. 94), which you can't miss. All of these attractions bring huge crowds of visitors. Stay on though after the sights close for the day and you can wander its pretty, low-rise streets, and drink and dine with the locals in peace. Belém's Avenida Brasília stretch of riverfront between the MAAT and the marina is home to a number of good-value and friendly seafood places. And it's in Belém that you'll find the original pastel de Belém — Portuguese custard tart — at Pastéis de Belém (see p. 100).

At the mouth of the Tejo estuary is Cascais, a white-washed fishing village, turn-of-the-century beach resort and posh suburb. Wander its densely knotted historic centre and eat seafood at one of its unpretentious restaurants like O Cantinho da Belinha (see p. 103), swim at Praia da Rainha or one of its other two beaches and clutch of rocky inlets, or strike out for the sweeping surf beaches around the headland, such as Guincho.

⇥ Praia da Rainha in Cascais

# 1 MOSTEIRO DOS JERÓNIMOS

Praça do Império, Belém
Mon–Sun 10.30am–6.30pm
(until 5.30pm in winter)
Tram 15, train Belém
[MAP p. 171 D3]

Overwhelming in its scale, its dripping decoration, its ambition, its crowds, Manuel I's limestone marvel is Lisbon's top must-see attraction. A paean to Portugal's Age of Discovery, this former Hieronymite Monastery houses explorer **Vasco da Gama's tomb**, and was where da Gama and his crew spent their last night before their momentous voyage to India in 1497. The huge maritime-themed late Gothic, early Renaissance mash-up was built over a century from 1501 and represents the culmination of Manueline design. Awe awaits, from the **Church of Santa Maria's** enchanted forest of columns, to the **cloisters**, with their intricate carved botanica, fantastical bestiary, nautical knots and anchors. The church's upper choir provides an excellent overview of all below or, for respite, head to the serene, little-visited **sacristy**, considered to be one of the best examples of 16th-century Portuguese craftsmanship, and lined with Indian–Portuguese cabinets and paintings.

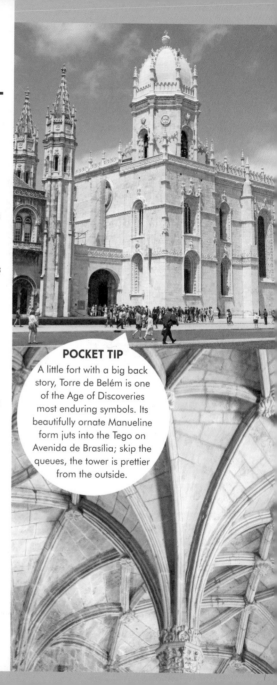

**POCKET TIP**

A little fort with a big back story, Torre de Belém is one of the Age of Discoveries most enduring symbols. Its beautifully ornate Manueline form juts into the Tego on Avenida de Brasília; skip the queues, the tower is prettier from the outside.

**POCKET TIP**

The Padrão dos Descobrimentos is an exuberant, if unsettling, celebration of Henry the Navigator and the explorers, sailors, soldiers and colonisers that set off around the world in his wake.

Museu Coleção Berardo
Arte Moderna e Contemporânea

# 2 MU*EU COLEÇÃO BERARDO

Centro Cultural de Belém
Praça do Império, Belém
Mon–Sun 10am–7pm
Tram 15E, train Belém
[MAP p. 170 C3]

The bold block structures of the Centro Cultural de Belém, the CCB, face off with the Mosteiro dos Jerónimos (*see* p. 94) across Praça do Império. The complex's star draw is the Museu Coleção Berardo, built to house billionaire Lisboeta José Berardo's astonishing collection. Its classic white cube architecture houses a Duchamp here, a Basquiat there. There's at least one temporary show of contemporary work and various curatorial interpretations of the collection, while two permanent exhibits chart works from each half of the 20th century, splitting at 1960: Mondrians and Mirós, then the Warhols and Judds. These permanent shows are curated to take the viewer on a chronological journey, making for a solid hit of highly pleasant art education. Coupled with the pizza and sushi-serving garden cafe, it's a joy for art-loving families with children.

# 3 CASA DAS HISTORIAS PAULA REGO

Avenida da República 300,
Cascais
Tues–Sun 10am–6pm
Train Cascais
[MAP p. 172 C3]

The Lisbon born, London Slade-trained artist Paula Rego is claimed by both Portugal and Britain as their own living treasure. Her monographic museum is a fascinating lure away from Cascais' sun and sardine strip. Rego was taught by painter Lucian Freud and exhibited with David Hockney in the '60s, and her often brutal, fairytale-inspired work has gone in and out of fashion many times. Here you can trace her long career from early vivid Abstraction to more recent narrative Figuration, via 22 iconic paintings and hundreds of works on paper. There are also paintings by her late husband, the English artist Victor Willing. The museum building was designed by Eduardo Souto de Moura, a Porto-based Pritzker Architecture Prize winner. Two pyramid-shaped towers conjure the traditional architecture of the region, and the earthy red concrete exterior contrasts with the interior's cool grey Cascais marble.

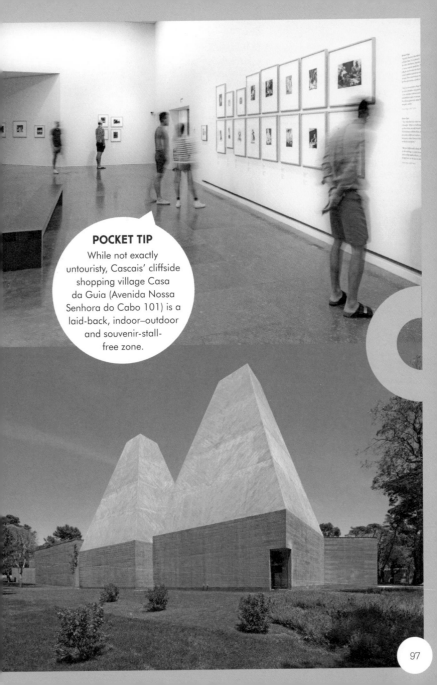

**POCKET TIP**
While not exactly untouristy, Cascais' cliffside shopping village Casa da Guia (Avenida Nossa Senhora do Cabo 101) is a laid-back, indoor–outdoor and souvenir-stall-free zone.

# 4 MUSEU DE ARTE, ARQUITETURA E TECNOLOGIA (MAAT)

Avenida Brasília, Belém
Wed–Mon 11am–7pm
Tram 15E, bus 720
[MAP p. 168 A2, 171 F3]

Right on the Rio Tejo (River Tagus), the multi-campus museum known as MAAT bridges the realms of technology, industrial history and contemporary art. Its sleek, low-slung 2016 Kunsthalle-style hub was designed by London architect Amanda Levete and its undulating form is covered in thousands of white, three-dimensional ceramic tiles. There are four mainly subterranean exhibition spaces devoted to temporary and commissioned shows. Even if you've no time to visit inside, the rooftop terrace will reward you with a beautiful perspective on the river. Further west, art installations fill what was once the city's main power station; an extraordinary, vast pavilion built in 1900 still houses all its original machinery. The space is often used for sound artworks, making for an even richer experience. Landscape architect Vladimir Djurovic's park joins the two.

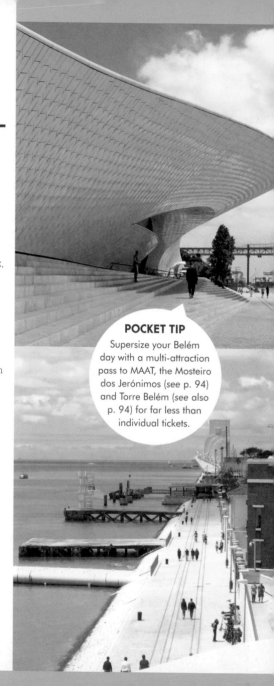

**POCKET TIP**
Supersize your Belém day with a multi-attraction pass to MAAT, the Mosteiro dos Jerónimos (see p. 94) and Torre Belém (see also p. 94) for far less than individual tickets.

# 5 DARWIN'S CAFÉ

Avenida Brasília Ala B, Belém
Mon 12.30pm–4pm, Tues–Sun
12.30pm–3.30pm, 7.30–11pm
Tram 15E, train Belém
[MAP p. 170 A4]

Scientists definitely do it better at this spectacular riverside restaurant reverently and riotously dedicated to perhaps the greatest of them all, Charles Darwin. As part of the architecturally interesting Champalimaud biomedical research centre, it occupies a strategic bump in the Rio Tejo (River Tagus) where the river widens to join the Atlantic. It might have once been all about the views, but the interior, with its circular leather booths and towering murals inspired by Darwin's original research drawings, is exhilarating too. Floor to (very high) ceiling windows still make sure that the river gets at least some of your attention, and on a summer's day the Tejo-facing deckchairs or umbrella shaded lounges on the terrace will definitely beckon. Locals come here for the reasonably priced, if not exactly authentic, risottos and pastas, as well as big salads, or there's a more formal menu if you want to make a special occasion of it. Innovative desserts, like mango carpaccio or rhubarb tart, are a highlight – even more so when taken on the terrace with a glass of Douro Valley espumante.

99

BELÉM & CASCAIS

# 6 PASTÉIS DE BELÉM

Rua de Belém 84-92, Belém
Mon–Sun 8am–11pm
Tram 15E, train Belém
[MAP p. 171 D3]

The pastel de Belém – a small, crisp, friable pastry shell, baked with a filling of rich yolky and spice-scented custard, and what's known outside the country as the Portuguese custard tart – enjoys adoration the world over. Pastéis de Belém is its alleged birthplace. The tart's origin story – one of out-of-work monks, sugar cane refiners, secret rooms and even more secret recipes in 1837 – is possibly not true and probably a case of canny early marketing, but it is as fascinating as the tarts are delicious. While they can be sampled all over the city, the crowds still come to Belém. These days the bakery churns out over 20,000 a day. Queues are the price you'll pay for your chance to sprinkle sugar and cinnamon, bite in and assess the hotly contested claim that these are Lisbon's finest (not to mention the rumour around town that it's pork fat in the shell that makes it so damn crispy). Queues to buy them and queues to sit and enjoy them. The faces of everyone post-pastel say that the bother of this pastry pilgrimage is well worth it.

100

# 7 TABERNA DOS FERREIROS

Taberna Ferreiros a Belém 5, Belém
Tues–Sun 12.30pm–11pm
Tram 15, train Belém
[MAP p. 171 E3]

Down a town alley, where the tour buses don't reach, this traditional taberna looks right out of central casting: pink marble-topped tables with dark wooden legs and an open kitchen up the back. That it's not as traditional as the decor would have you believe, won't become clear until your dishes appear. Chef Maurilhio Fernandes' menu offers staples like bacalhau and bife (and prices commensurate with taberna dining), but these arrive pared back and plated with a not-so-traditional attention to detail. Then there are Mediterranean-inspired dishes, like a squid ink linguini, a Peruvian ceviche or two, and dishes which declare culinary neutrality, like sausage with wilted wild greens or squid with lemon and herbs. Don't worry: peixinhos da horta (tempura-like vegetable fritters) are always on – though change seasonally – and perfect for a post-sightseeing snack, with one of the cold climate white wines from Cores de Chima's Alentejo Atlantic coast vineyards. Staff will happily welcome you between lunch and dinner sittings.

## POCKET TIP

Splash out for drinks at the poolside Atlântico bar at Oitavos (Rua de Oitavos), a five-star hotel, or at the venerable dining room at the Cimas English Bar (Avenida Marginal) on a pretty stretch of coast in Estoril.

## 8 O CANTINHO DA BELINHA

Avenida Vasco da Gama 133, Cascais
Casa dos Pescadores
[MAP p. 172 C2]

Fish feasts always taste better eaten on sea-green check tablecloths beneath dusty hanging frigates. Model ship lovers, sardine fanatics and anyone with nostalgia for the sea will love this courtyard canteen, part of the Associação De Armadores e Pescadores De Cascais (Shipowners and Fisherfolks' Association). A little out of the pretty knot of the historic centre, you'll find cheap prices and cheerful staff ready to share where each catch is from. Yes, they have sardines – you'll smell them on arrival. They're joined by a long list of fish that will be chargrilled; less glamourous varieties like mackerel are a steal. Or try the chaputa frita – Atlantic pomfrit steaks – with Brazilian-style rice and black beans. Everything comes with an oil and vinegar doused salad – iceberg lettuce, sliced cucumber, grated beets and carrot – and chips or boiled potatoes. There's a meat menu, with back-to-basics fare like bistoque (steak, egg, rice and potato), burgers, schnitzels and chops.

**POCKET TIP**
For an afternoon coffee or casual sunset drink, head to the little cliffside Largo da Praia da Rainha above Cascais' beach of the same name, where there are a few easy outdoor bars with views to choose from.

103

# ALMADA &
# COSTA CAPARICA

In a city dominated by its riverfront, it's hard not to gaze and ponder what lies on the other side. Luckily, it's an easy urge to indulge as Lisbon's southside, in fact not Lisbon at all, but the distinct municipality of Almada, is but a swift ferry ride (see p. 107) from the centre. As you disembark over the river, just by the wharf is a restaurant-lined square, and a web of winding streets unfolds in the village of Cacilhas, which feels like the traditional fishing village it once was. The riverfront here is also a draw for street art and graffiti fans, its post-industrial landscape being the perfect canvas. Eschewing public transport, a cheap Uber across the Ponte 25 de Abril, (25 April Bridge, see p. 106) will get you to the other side too and, like the ferry, also delivers breathtaking views. Above Cacilhas, from where you can climb the stairs or take the Elevador da Boca do Vento, is Cristo Rei (see p. 106), the city's most visible landmark.

Further south, and due west is Costa Caparica. This beautiful surf beach's stretch of concrete boardwalk, old-school restaurants and grid of mid-century apartment blocks has always been beloved by locals for weekend fun, but often overlooked by visitors in favour of Cascais' historic centre and posh gated resorts. Still relatively untouristed, it is currently reinventing itself, with an influx of expats, surfers and those seeking a laid-back beach lifestyle. Fabulous places to eat, drink, watch the beach breaks and be merry, like Dr. Bernard (see p. 110) and Posto 9 (see p. 113) are the new spirit of place. It doesn't take long to get back to nature here either – just beyond the beach umbrellas lay an utterly beguiling 13 kilometres (8 miles) of ancient dunes and cliffs, scented pine forests and coastal plains: the Arriba Fóssil (see p. 108), the protected Fossil Coast.

→ Benfica football club fan car in Costa Caparica

**SIGHTS**
1. Cristo Rei
2. Cacilhas Ferry
3. Arriba Fóssil

**EATING & DRINKING**
4. Ponto Final
5. Dr. Bernard
6. Kurika Cervejaria
7. Posto 9

E PLURIBUS UNUM

O BARBAS

# 1 CRISTO REI

Avenida Cristo Rei, Alto do
Pragal, Almada
Mon–Sun 9.30am–6.30pm
Ferry Cacilhas, bus 101
[MAP p. 168 C4]

The 110 metre-high (360 feet)
Cristo Rei, Lisbon's hovering,
holy mascot, sits by the Ponte
25 de Abril (25 April Bridge)
and makes for a particularly
ethereal sight when flood-lit
at night. Built with reverent
gratitude for divine protection
of the nation during World
War II, Cristo Rei was
inaugurated in the deeply
conservative days of 1959.
What it lacks in elegance, it
more than makes up for with
presence: set on an arched
plinth that tilts towards each
point of the compass, with
Christ's open arms visible
throughout the city. Most
remarkable of all though, Christ
was hand-carved in situ,
100 metres up (328 feet). The
lift up to the viewing terrace
represents, for pious visitors,
the ascension into heaven,
while the 59 steps up the final
few metres mark the effort
of transcending an earthly
life. There's a **bar** and a **cafe**
once you're back from the
firmament; join pilgrims for a
beverage. Otherwise, you're
a short stroll from Cacilhas'
bountiful **cervejarias**
(seafood-focused beerhalls) on
the riverfront.

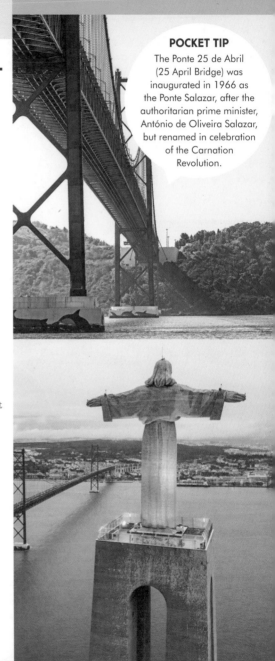

**POCKET TIP**

The Ponte 25 de Abril
(25 April Bridge) was
inaugurated in 1966 as
the Ponte Salazar, after the
authoritarian prime minister,
António de Oliveira Salazar,
but renamed in celebration
of the Carnation
Revolution.

## 2 CACILHA∫ FERRY

Terminal Fluvial (Cais do Sodré ferry terminal), Rua da Cintura do Porto de Lisboa
Mon–Sun 5.20am–1.30am
[MAP p. 169 F3]

This workaday commuter service vessel's interiors have seen better days, but it's still one of the city's cheapest and most satisfying attractions. The journey across the river is a brief 10 to 15 minutes and is a direct one, but it gives you a spectacular view of the Ponte 25 de Abril (25 April Bridge, *see* p. 106) and Baixa, especially at sunset on fine days when the sun sinks behind the bridge in a tangerine explosion. As it's a commuter service, it's best to avoid early morning and late afternoon peak hours. The single fare of €1.30 can be charged to your Viagem card (*see* p. 146) and note that there's no return fare, so charge up two single ones unless you're going to make a night of it. The Cais do Sodré ferry terminal is just south of the train station, in its own pavilion.

**POCKET TIP**
Another pretty ferry route is the Belém–Trafaria–Porto Brandão service; it is however a longer trip and departs less frequently than the one to Cacilhas.

# 3 ARRIBA FÓSSIL

Rua Dom João V 17, Aroeira
Transpraia Fonte de Telha
[MAP p. 174 B2]

You could be forgiven for heading to Costa Caparica for a dip and seafood lunch, and entirely missing this natural wonder. But just beyond the boardwalks, the Fossil Coast's stretch of cliffs, officially known as the Paisagem Protegida da Arriba Fóssil da Costa de Caparica, are Western Europe's most extraordinary example of Pliocene period sedimentary rock strata: far more stunning to see than it may sound. The 13 kilometres (8 miles) of unusual towering, ridged forms, some at over 70 metres (230 feet) high – eroded by the wind over thousands of years – are at their most beautiful at dusk, when it becomes a glowing wall of gold and rust. There are also stone pine, mastic and eucalyptus forests to hike (these were planted after the 1755 earthquake to protect farmland from the ever-encroaching dunes). Touring here is best done in your own car, or with a jeep tour from Lisbon. You can, however, get here on the Transpraia, a *Noddy*-style train connecting the strip's resorts. The far southern terminus is in the small enclave of Fonte da Telha, which will put you in the middle of the protected area.

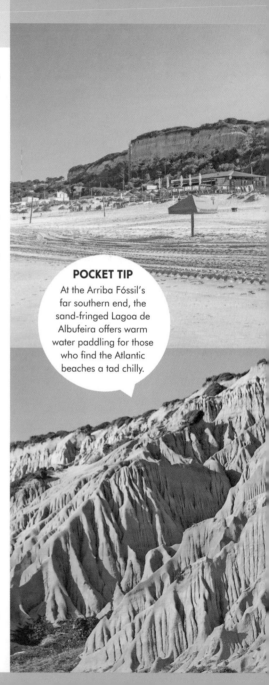

**POCKET TIP**
At the Arriba Fóssil's far southern end, the sand-fringed Lagoa de Albufeira offers warm water paddling for those who find the Atlantic beaches a tad chilly.

# 4 PONTO FINAL

Rua do Ginjal 72, Almada
212 760 743
Wed–Mon 12.30pm–4.30pm,
7–11pm
Ferry Cacilhas
[MAP p. 169 E4]

Along from the ferry wharf, towards the mouth of the river and past the picturesquely crumbling warehouses, you'll find this ridiculously scenic (and definitely not-so-secret) restaurant and bar. Waterfront dining, a view of the bridge, and everyday prices make it worth the ferry ride even if you're not up for exploring further. Match pão Alentejo (country sourdough) with Évora sheep's milk cheese, order a flaky cod and chickpea or octopus salad to share and then tuck into platters of the catch of the day, say grilled sardines or red mullet. When it's cooler, the carapauzinhos (little 'horse' mackerel) with tomato rice is warming. If you're dining with a group, try one of the special Angolan dishes, a spicy chicken muamba stew or curry. Outside tables – and it's all about the outside here – should be grabbed early, with gusto, or booked ahead.

**RESTAURANTE PONTO FINAL**

## POCKET TIP

Can't snag a table at Ponto Final or it's Tuesday when it's closed? Try cute Atira-te ao Rio next door for more simple Portuguese dishes and views.

# 5 DR. BERNARD

Praia do CDS, Apoio de Praia 11
Sun–Mon 9am–8pm, Wed–Sat
9am–12am (May–Oct)
[MAP p. 174 A1]

Don't think of Dr. Bernard as just a restaurant. The airy pavilion's rustic wood, bright daubed beams, potted palms and French film posters give it a sense of occasion but there are also hammocks and cushions for morning coffee before a surf or a glass of natural, small-producer wine after a swim. Local and expat surfers (French owned, it's a favourite of the local French community) pop by to discuss the day's swell, there are drop-in yoga and pilates classes and DJs on the weekends. That said, you'll also eat very well here indeed – the kitchen is care of a new pop-up chef each season and, while some things will change, the menu will always feature the best local fish and seafood done in simple, innovative ways. All this, plus surf, sand and horizon from every window. Come for lunch and you may find yourself making plans to spend an *entire* summer here.

**POCKET TIP**

Just across the road from the restaurant, Dr. Bernard has a handful of stylish, pared-back rooms for beach and wellness stays.

# 6 KURIKA CERVEJARIA

Rua Capitão Leitão 34A,
Almada
[MAP p. 169 D4]

A true southside local's cervejaria (seafood-focused beerhall), Kurika is lots of no-fuss fun. During prime time, such as Sunday lunch and dinner, you'll probably have to wait for a table, and most summer evenings too, but it's never too long and never too harried. English-speaking staff will help you with the menu, a straight up best-of cervejaria favourites, like prawns with rice, clams in garlic, grilled crab, a generous bitoque (steak, egg, rice and sauté potatoes) or omelettes, and a legendary prego (steak sandwich). If you're not sure what to order, look at what the next table is having and go with it. Beer flows and dangerously affordable wine comes by the half bottle carafe or bottle.

**POCKET TIP**

Petisqueira Nana (Rua Eugénio Salvador 23, Charneca de Caparica) is known for its traditional dishes in a suburban shaded courtyard; serves are mostly under €10 and favourites like fried chicken, stuffed gizzards or octopus salad come in half serves.

# 7 POƧTO 9

Praia do Rei
Mon–Sun 9am–11pm
(Apr–Oct), Sat–Sun 9am–11pm
only (Nov–Mar)
[MAP p. 174 B2]

Head south towards Fonte da Telha from Costa Caparica's centre and you'll come across this Mediterranean-style beach club, complete with whitewashed beach shacks, white rattan furniture and a forest of beach umbrellas on the sand. A perfect beach bum menu takes you from morning croissants and omelettes to a Franco–Portuguese lunch, apéro and dinners. Rillettes and radishes sit beside choco frito, a Setubal specialty of crispy fried cuttlefish, there's gazpacho, burgers and salads, and fish or chicken grills, delightfully served with ratatouille. Beach club days become club nights during high summer, with 4am finishes – check their Facebook page or website Resident Advisor for the DJ schedule. Francophiles take note: Provencal rosé is served by the bottle or glass.

113

# FIELD TRIP

# ∫INTRA & THE COA∫T

Impossibly fertile forested hills, a collection of fairytale architecture and ancient Celtic mystery sites roused the imagination of composer Richard Strauss and poet Lord Byron, who called it a 'glorious Eden'. The much-bandied 'Disneyland for grownups' moniker is true: the town of Sintra really does feel like it's under an enchantment. Designed along high Romantic lines, mostly by German architects, the palaces were built for the Portuguese royals to showcase their imperial wealth and boast layers of influences, imagination and abandon. The precious detail of Palácio Nacional de Sintra (*see* p. 116), Palácio da Pena's gleeful splendour (*see* p. 116) and the mysterious gardens of the Quinta da Regaleira (*see* p. 117) are not to be missed.

Just as soul stirring (and a lot less crowded) is the Sintra Coast (*see* p. 117), ten minutes' drive west through beautifully bucolic country and the Sintra-Cascais Natural Park. Sheer cliffs drop to the majestic Atlantic Ocean, whitewashed fishing villages like Azenhas do Mar (*see* p. 118) vertiginously overlook calm coves, and hairpin stairs descend to secret surf breaks. Here too, is Cabo da Roca (*see* p. 117), mainland Europe's most westerly point, a place as intensely beautiful as it is symbolic. Restaurants draw the seafood-loving Lisboeta for their unequalled fresh aquatic produce.

Two train routes travel to Sintra from Lisbon in under 40 minutes; the most convenient is from central Rossio, the other is from Oriente and these run at least every 30 minutes. Hop-on, hop-off bus 435 takes you from the station into Sintra-Vila. Daytrippers arrive in great numbers so staying overnight in Sintra (*see* p. 122) or on the coast or surrounding countryside, will afford you peace in the early mornings and come nightfall.

→ *Palácio Nacional de Sintra*

**POCKET TIP**

Hidden among rocky outcrops in a forest above town, the cork-lined cells and chapels of the former Convent of the Capuchos are fascinating to explore. Built in the 16th century, its architecture is of nature worshipping and pious humility, a stark contrast to Sintra's opulent palaces.

## SINTRA-VILA

The entire centre of the town of Sintra is a UNESCO World Heritage Site and a complete sight in itself. You could wander the hills and hike the forests without visiting anywhere in particular and still be overcome by the town's magical spell. But each of the main sites has its own unique backstory and appeal.

The **Palácio Nacional de Sintra** began life as a medieval Moorish castle and its Mudéjar (post-reconquest Iberian–Islamic style) bones and later Manueline (Portuguese late Gothic) touch-ups mesh in what is Portugal's most well-preserved medieval castle. Two massive conical chimneys are a startling feature and are today seen as a symbol of the town. Inside it's a dreamy confection of tiles, columns and courtyards, mosaics and murals.

The pastel towers of **Palácio da Pena** are just a taste of the Rhineish fantasy built for Dom Ferdinand II by a Prussian architect in 1840, and one of the most complete expressions of Romanticism in the world. The ornamental exterior is matched inside by a giddy mix of stucco and trompe l'oeil, statuary and frescos. Look out for the reception room with its Islamic palace trompe l'oeil of vaulted ceilings and botanica. The **gardens**, some 200 lush

116

hectares (494 acres), have labyrinthine paths and are planted with exotic trees from around the world, none more so than the fabulous Feteira da Rainha (Queen's Fern Garden), which drips in antipodean ferns and tree ferns.

The **Quinta da Regaleira**, a latecomer built in 1910, was the private residence of a coffee baron. His neo-Manueline house and chapel, an intricate folly of towers and moss-covered walls, can be explored in 10 minutes, but it's the gardens here that will threaten to never let you go. Whimsical decoration and winding paths hide a network of deep grottos, tunnels and mysterious follies, all of which are underpinned by occult teachings. Not least of the mysteries are the wells and inverted towers which hint at Dante and Masonic initiation rites, and, in fact, bear the Knights Templar cross.

## ſINTRA COAST

Until the 14th century, most Europeans thought that **Cabo da Roca** was the edge of the world and its windswept desolation still feels deliciously remote. There's little here in the austere gale-resistant scrubland beyond the still operational **Farol de Cabo da Roca** (Portugal's first lighthouse, dating to 1772),

some ambitious walking trails and a monument bearing a quote from poet Luis Camoes: 'where the land ends and the sea begins'.

To the north, **Azenhas do Mar**'s white and blue painted houses circle down a steep cliff-face to a perfect curve of sand. Considered one of the most picturesque coastal towns in Portugal, its graceful, sleepy streets are lovely for ambling; there are some more serious walks around the town and cliffs, or you can swim in the stunningly sited ocean pool.

South of here the road hugs the coast and drops into **Praia Grande**, a grand strip of sand indeed. It's a favourite with surfers and each August hosts the world boarding championships.

There's a scantily marked but spectacular hiking trail from Praia Grande to **Praia da Adraga** (the trail actually begins in **Praia das Maças**, the easiest of the beaches to access) or you can drive inland and then back out to the coast again. With its sharply jutting rock formations, rocky arch rising from the sand and sea-hazed horizons, utterly wild Adraga might just be the most beautiful beach you've ever seen.

Each summer, the endearing 1930 tram cars of the **Electrico de Sintra** trundle from downtown Sintra 13 kilometres

(8 miles) to the often busy but undoubtedly beautiful little town of **Maças**. The tram only runs from Friday to Sunday and gets very busy in high summer, so plan accordingly (out of season, just jump on the bus which runs the same route).

## ∫INTRA EATING & DRINKING

Sintra-Vila's pretty cobblestone streets can feel overwhelmed by the great number of visitors, with tacky souvenir stalls and restaurant spruikers at odds with the atmosphere. But it's not hard to strike out and wander beyond the main tourist trails, to corners where the town retains a gently bohemian, fittingly eccentric edge.

**Café Saudade** (Avenida Dr. Miguel Bombarda 6), once a bakery which turned out Sintra's signature pastry, the queijada (a shortcrust pastry tart with a baked cheesecake-like filling), Saudade now has a good daytime menu of casual dishes and is a great place to settle in with an early evening wine. It also hosts exhibitions and live music.

**Villa Craft Beer & Bread** (Rua Paço 12) is another casual (and affordable) place. It occupies an old terrace on a steep street just near the Palácio Nacional de Sintra (*see* p. 116) and has a huge selection

### POCKET TIP

The Sintra Coast has some of Portugal's most consistent surfing conditions, with glassy beach breaks for beginners in summer and varied, challenging waves for the pros in winter.

of Portuguese craft beer, including the Sintra-brewed blondes, stouts and weissbiers from Rafeira and also bakes its own bread; buy a loaf or try it with various toppings from chorizo to bachalu (saltcod). Next door **Botica Saloia** (Rua Paço 16) has a similar vibe and does tapas dishes (look out for the Negrais piglet) and wines from the Lisbon region and Colares DOC, while vegetarian and vegan cantine **A Praça** (Rua Paço 16) serves beautiful salads, soups, dips, cakes and desserts.

Old tearoom **A Raposa** (Rua Conde Ferreira 29) feels straight from a Merchant Ivory film but below its handpainted celestial ceiling serves up dishes with a nicely modern sensibility. While you're in town don't forget to order a queijada with your coffee, or pick up a pack to take-away – you'll soon be craving these over pastel de nata (Portuguese custard tart).

## SINTRA COAST EATING & DRINKING

There's no shortage of restaurants with ocean views on headlands and beach promenades, and simple menu of freshly caught seafood so it's hard to go wrong.

Stylish, pale wood-clad **Azenhas do Mar** (below Rua João Alves de Freitas, Azenhas do Mar) sits below

the cliff in the village of the same name, right on the sea, and is one of the region's most beloved for blow-out feasts of freshly speared fish grilled in salt, stuffed crab or goose barnacles caught locally. Book ahead in high summer (and bring your swimming things to take advantage of the sea pool).

Back up in the village centre of Azenhas do Mar, unsigned **Cafe das Patricias** (Rua da Casa Rita 1) does one of the best polvo alagereiro (octopus and potatoes in olive oil) around, with octopus that's hand-caught locally (and hand delivered) each day.

Down the coast road, the stellar views and faultless seafood continue at **Nortada** (Avenida Alfredo Coelho 8), where the usual wood and red table cloth aesthetic has been updated with a slick white and blue fit-out.

**Bar do Fondo** (Avenida Alfredo Coelho) gives you front row seats right on the stunning Praia Grande (see p. 118) and it's an unbelievably romantic spot for sunset drinks and simple seafood dishes.

The coast was once known for its vineyards, and a few remain. **Colares**, just a few miles inland, produces complex aged reds and rich, herbal whites from some of the oldest pre-phylloxera vines in Europe (the Adega Regional de Colares happens to be the

# ∫INTRA ε THE COA∫T

**POCKET TIP**

Seafood-weary? Moinho Iberico (Avenida Moinhos do Arneiro 98, Magoito) cooks top-quality steaks over an open flame inside an old windmill. If you're game try their other speciality: lagarto, or Iberian 'lizards', a long pork loin strip for lovers of densely marbled meat.

oldest wine cooperative in the country, founded in 1931 and the Colares appellation dates back to 1908).

**Casal de Santa Maria**
(Rua Principal 18/20, Casas Novas-Colares) makes wine from grapes grown in the most westerly vineyards of mainland Europe on sandy soil; it welcomes visitors to taste the unique maritime vintages.

## ∫INTRA ∫LEEPING

Family run guesthouse **Águamel**, set in a beautiful 1885 townhouse, and sweetly kooky **Chalet Saudade** (Rua Dr. Alfredo da Costa 23) are lovely finds in a town where places can be twee.

**Lawrence's** (Rua Consiglieri Pedroso 38) is the oldest operating hotel in the Iberian peninsula (Byron took a bed here). Rooms are classically styled with floral curtains and four posters but are light and airy, with treetop-filled windows and floorboards.

Head up into the hills ten minutes' south of town for the full European resort experience at **Penha Longa** (Estrada da Lagoa Azul, Linhó Sintra), with two golf courses, spa, indoor and outdoor pools, six restaurants and spacious rooms.

**Almáa Sintra Hostel**
(Caminho dos Frades 1) swaps drinking games and good times for peace and quiet. Rooms are

austere but calming, sheets are organic cotton and there are acres of gardens to relax in, including an Olympic-sized irrigation tank for swimming.

## SINTRA COAST SLEEPING

The sea views of a few of the coast's hotels only just balance out their creaky surrounds. Luckily there are a couple of notable exceptions.

**Outpost Arribas** (Rua Dr. António Brandão de Vasconcelos, Azenhas do Mar) is one of the most lovely places to stay in the whole region and a destination in itself. Once a historical family home built in an intriguing Portuguese–Modernist blend by local architect Raul Lino in the 1940s, this mini-resort has five spacious apartments. Each is filled with beautifully handcrafted furniture and locally-sourced rugs, while retaining features of the original house, from grand stone fireplaces to dark wood staircases. The house sits on the cliffs just north of Azenhas do Mar (*see* p. 118), with the mighty Atlantic crashing on the rocks below, a rambling garden, pool, tennis courts and a vegetable patch.

A little inland, **Azen Cool House** (Avenida Nossa Sra. da Esperança 308) has good value rooms which look out into the evergreen countryside with a pool, bikes and ping-pong.

# COMPORTA

Wedged between the broad Sado estuary and the crashing Atlantic, a little over an hour from Lisbon, is the Herdade da Comporta – a region of beaches, waterways, ricefields and forests surrounding a village of the same name. Storks stand sentinel, their nests precariously heaped on telegraph poles, on chimneys and in trees. All is enveloped in a dreamy hush of patchwork rice fields and salt pans, where fishing huts on stilts line up along tranquil waterways, horses graze, flamingoes wade and bottleneck dolphins frolic. The villages, Comporta itself, as well as Carvalhal, Possanco, Torre and Carrasqueira, are today dotted with barefoot-chic shops, cute cafes and rustic restaurants, but their streetscapes of low-slung white daub, thatch houses and farm buildings still hark back to their old fishing and rice growing days.

Snow white beaches trail down the coast, protected by deep dunes, and are fringed with forests of umbrella pine and cork oak. Owned for 50 years by one of Portugal's wealthiest banking families, and protected by its status as nature reserve, the region has escaped the development that mars Portugal's south coast. Instead, villas are secreted deep in the forests and belong to Europe's haute creatives, including German painter Anslem Keiffer and designer Philippe Starck. But don't let a stealth wealth reputation put you off, whatever your budget. Low-key resorts like Sublime Comporta (see p. 132) are generous in their offerings, there are plenty of well-priced rentals outside high season, eating out is casual, and surfing, sunbaking and soaking in the pine-scented silence are free.

Comporta is just over an hour's drive from central Lisbon and best explored by car. Private transfers are possible, but public transport is tricky, involving catching the train to Setúbal, then the catamaran or car ferry to Troia and a taxi.

→ *Pêgo beach, Comporta*

## BEACHE∫ & NATURE

Beach snobs: there's nothing to fear, as the 60 kilometres (37 miles) of pristine white sand coastline will not disappoint. Sparsely dotted with small villages, all discreetly tucked away beyond the dunes, the only human incursion into the wild, brine-swept expanses are the clutches of beach umbrellas and loungers in high season, and the occasional beach shack restaurant or bar. Even these have a driftwood impermanence, a sense they could be swallowed up by the sand at any moment. In between, the beaches stretch on and on, unspoilt and unpeopled.

**Praia Comporta**, Comporta's home beach, is just over the rice paddies from the village. It's a favoured spot for an evening drink, its carpark fills in summer and its supervised swimming zone can mean the sand can also get crowded, but for most of the time it's serene as can be. Head down to **Praia Carvalhal** for the exquisitely preserved dune ecosystem, in spring it's a riot of flowers and insect life. Between these two, accessible only by bike or foot, is **Praia dos Brejos**, a completely unadorned and often deserted strip of sand.

**Praia do Pego**'s four kilometre (2.5 mile) stretch is considered one of the most beautiful in

Europe and feels the most remote of the main beaches.

To the far north, the gentle waves of **Praia Tróia Galé** and **Praia Tróia** are great for families, although its easy access via catamaran from Setúbal sees a larger influx of daytrippers than the other beaches, and it has the most development.

Out of the water, there's kayaking in the rice irrigation channels, forest walking and horseriding on the beach. Excursions include boat trips out to sea or across the **Sado estuary** or to the 16th-century **Convento de Santa Maria da Arrábida**, or a potter about the **Roman ruins at Cetobriga** up on the Tróia peninsula – but the main attraction really is the coast itself.

**POCKET TIP**

As for the rest of the coast of central Portugal, the water temperature ranges from around 14–20°C (57–68°F), that is, refreshing on hot summer days, but otherwise downright chilly.

## EATING & DRINKING

If you've got a hunch that seafood and rice dominate menus around these parts, then you'd be deliciously right.

The **Museu do Arroz** (N 261), a traditional restaurant that's part of Comporta village's former rice mill, serves up the flavoursome local specialty of cuttlefish, monkfish rice and squid ink rice, as well as rustic Alentejo pork and eggs scrambled with farinheira, a local smoked sausage. Eat in the lofty beamed 1950s

127

warehouse or out on the waterside terrace.

In the heart of Comporta village head to chic **Cavalariça** (Rua do Secador 9), set in an old stable, for innovative international and local dishes, including inspired desserts and cocktails.

There are also plentiful places for those whose taste or budget calls for simpler things. Call in for a €2 bifana or prego (meat sandwich), a beer and a chat with local workers at Comporta village's **Cafetaria do Talho** (Rua do Comércio 7) or sip smoothies at the smart, sandy **Colmo Bar** (Largo de São João 3). **Arado** (Rua Pedro Nunes 6) does a great take on the dive bar, with a staggering list of gins to try. Sweet little bakery, **Eucalyptus** (Rua do Comércio 1) serves up tarts, salads, juices and burgers on its terrace or get take-away for a beach or forest picnic. In summer there's always street eat pop-ups, like **Piadina Zanotta** (Largo de São João).

**Sublime Comporta's** (*see* p. 132) beautiful contemporary restaurant **Sem Porta** (N 261 1, Grândola), literally without doors, which it indeed is, has a menu of earthy but lyrical dishes: tomato, strawberry and mint salad is served with its house-pressed olive oil; roast turbot, cockles and coriander come with the comfort of grits; and the fresh pop of cucumber and apple highlights

the richness of suckling pig terrine and oysters. In summer, book ahead for the **Food Circle**, an extraordinary chef's table dining experience set in among the green bounty of the restaurant's kitchen garden, where cooking is done only with fire.

Set right on the beach at Praia del Pego, **Sal** is a local's favourite for perfect fried calamari and fish soup that's just as pleasing as the view, and the blond wood and canvas canopies of the surrounds. More traditional seafood rice dishes are on the menu at homey **Dona Bica** (N 261), down the road in Torre.

## ЅHOPPING

Boho, beachy, carefree: Comporta has spawned its very own style, in the manner of Ibiza or Bali. Comporta's little blue and white village is home to a number of shops that capture this enviable lifestyle.

Right at the roundabout, is **Lavanda** (Largo de São João 3), with what must be one of the world's most extensive range of straw hats, as well as beach dresses, linen shirts and upmarket accessories.

Owned by the people behind the Museu do Arroz (*see* p. 127), shop **A Loja do Museu do Arroz** (Largo de São João 8) has a lovely ramble of rooms to explore,

stuffed with bold jewellery and objects sourced globally, gauzy Indian cotton shirts and smocks, a small vintage fashion collection, and intriguing decorative pieces, like early 20th-century posters from Brazil.

**Côté Sud** (Beco das Comportas 2) is the local go-to for bikinis and floaty beach tunics, boardshorts and raffia bags.

The beach outpost of Lisbon designer Teresa Martin, **TM Collection** (Largo São João 3), offers up her especially designed resort-wear, while **Manumaya Made with Love** (Largo da São João 8) ramps up the colour (and affordability) with vivid ceramics, hand-embroidered dresses and striped ponchos made in the owner's home country of Guatemala.

In summer, head to the **Casa da Cultura** (Rua do Secador 8), where a dozen or so pop-up 'shacks' are collected together in an old cinema and the adjacent rice barn. There's also a program of exhibitions in the **Cinema Room**.

Those wanting to replicate the local look should browse the homewares and furniture at **Rice** (Rua do Secador 8), while vintage enthusiasts will enjoy the mid-century collections of **Vintage Department** (Rua do Secador 5).

For those who prefer their souvenirs to be edible, **Mercearia Gomes** (Rua do

Secador 14) is a bountiful grocery store selling local rice, cheese, sardines, oils, soaps, wines and fresh, seasonal produce. Even if you're not up for a food shop, its floor-to-ceiling shelves are a visual delight.

The region's other villages have some gems, including little whitewashed **Barracuda Comporta** (Av 18 de Dezembro 1) in Carvalhal's sleepy main street, with a truly unique and aesthetically thrilling collection of vintage furniture and remodelled pieces (like, a Scottish 19th-century chair upholstered in rare West African cloth). There are also bright and affordable glassware and ceramics for the table.

Look out for the **stalls along the N 261** road selling gorgeous raffia bags, colourful totes and eminently packable locally made rag rugs.

## SLEEPING

For many years, Comporta and the coast's small stock of places to stay were traded between friends and family by word-of-mouth. Now, everyone can be part of the clique via reasonably priced cabanas or villas. A small handful of boutique resorts have recently popped up and there are good shoulder season discounts to be found.

At **Sublime Comporta**
(N 261 1, Grândola) a gentle
scattering of wooden cabins
and villas sit in a wildflower-
strewn old cork plantation. An
airy contemporary pavilion
houses a restaurant, and there's
a pretty pool or a lagoon-like
natural swimming hole to
cool off in. A spa area has an
indoor pool and there are tennis
courts, bikes to borrow and
weekly wellness activities.
Couple-perfect cabins come
with crisp sheets, big baths and
retreat-like forest views. There
are multi-bedroom compounds
to share with family or friends
to make it more affordable. An
owner's suite occupies the top
floor of the original house, with
big rough-rendered balconies
overlooking the pool. Woody
but elegant eco-cabins each
have their own front deck built
out over the natural pool's
reedy banks.

**Silent Living** provides
guests with the experience
of original beach shacks and
old fishermen's huts, now
done up in a meditative mix
of rush matting and white
linen but still calling on the
old fisherman's style of the
area. **Casas na Areia**'s (Sítio
da Carrasqueira) compound
structure – four separate units
house a living and cooking
space, as well as bedrooms
and ensuites – feels as if it's
from another time. Dine with
your feet in the sand – quite
literally, as the dining room has
a sand floor, another tradition

transformed. The **Cabanas No Rio** (Sítio da Carrasqueira) is two tiny cabins, one with an ensuite bedroom, the other for living, facing out into the vastness of the river, with nature's own theatre in front of you, a cast of storks and flamingoes, and the odd cameo from the estuary dolphins.

At **Quinta** (Rua de Alto de Pina 2), rooms overlooking the pool and rice paddies feature traditional cane furniture, curved headboards, woven baskets and bold textiles, but are otherwise stripped back. The palette is one of earthy minimalism, even in the pool area and spa: a calming symphony of black, white and natural tones.

Mid-range eco-resorts abound, including the cabins of **Cocoon** (Parcela 105, Quinta do Sossego, Muda), set in a grassy, pine-dotted garden with its own lagoon or the folky **A Serenada Enoturismo** (RIC 1265, Outeiro André, Grândola).

More budget-friendly guesthouses and farmstays can be found in the hills a 30-minute drive from the coast in hamlets like Grândola. **Sobreiras** (Alentejo Country Hotel; Caixa Postal 3143, Mosqueirões) has a cluster of stylish, simple wooden cabins set around a pool that overlooks rugged countryside, just a short drive from the region's wild southern beaches.

133

## FIELD TRIP

# PORTO

Historic Porto, both a Celtic and Roman city, and then Portugal's great ship building centre of the 15th century, has an unmistakable old-world grace, the compelling remnants of 20th-century industrial grit and a bubbling, creative, cool present. It's hard not to talk about the country's second city without conjuring comparisons to Lisbon and without courting rivalries. The locals certainly do, rather a lot. But don't bother to compare: this city is its own sweet, very happening, very good looking, self.

Sights, from the centre's Art Nouveau wonder, the São Bento train station (*see* p. 138), azulejo tile-clad Igreja de Santo Ildefonso (*see* p. 138) and the outstanding Museum of Contemporary Art at the Serralves Foundation (*see* p. 139) are worth your time, but this city's most enduring appeal is in the pleasures of everyday good living. It is a city with a hugely exciting culture of innovation. Restaurants like Oficina (*see* p. 141) showcase hearty local produce and spectacular northern Portuguese wines (including, of course, Port) and shops such as Coração Alecrim (*see* p. 137) mix vintage nous with beautiful artisan work, and add in a sustainable cafe too. There's contemporary architecture to admire, not least of all the stunning Casa da Música (*see* p. 139) and a booming gallery and design scene, one where, handily, most of the city's galleries are within a few blocks of each other.

Express trains from Lisbon's Santa Apolónia station make it here in just over two and a half hours, or it's around three hours by car, so it's doable for an ambitious daytrip. It's far better though to devote one or two nights (*see* p. 142) to explore its eating opportunities and nightlife more fully, head to the upmarket beachy enclave of Foz or to do wine tastings, walking or river cruising in the nearby Douro Valley.

→ *Traditional azulejos-clad building in Porto*

**POCKET TIP**

Boat cruises head up the Douro Valley from Porto or you can take the scenic train to Pinhão and explore from there.

## SIGHTS

You'll probably start your Porto wandering in **Ribeira**, the city's UNESCO-listed centre, which is packed with sights, places to eat and drink, and, inevitably, other travellers. Nothing is very far (although there are occasional hills to tackle) and a short walk north-west will put you in the vibrant **Design District** (see p. 139). Views can be had at the city's 12th-century Romanesque **cathedral**. The walk through the twisted medieval streets from Ribeira's Avenida Dom Afonso Henriques, to its hilltop lookout is almost as interesting as the church's rose windows and Gothic cloisters. Decompress in the **Jardim do Palácio de Cristal**, with more stunning views.

In the other direction is **Bolhão**, another easygoing inner city local area with the city's fabulous market. Salt-licked **Foz**, out along the river, where the Douro River meets the Atlantic Ocean, is a fashionable but atmospheric little suburb, known for its fabulous eating options – it's a short ride there on tram 1 or bus 500.

Get your bearings and fall in love with the city stretched before you with a stroll across the **Ponte de Dom Luís I**. Porto's most recognisable landmark is not just a useful way in which to cross to the other side of the broad Douro,

it's a stunning piece of 19th-century industrial architecture and the work of a Gustave Eiffel student. It also offers some of the city's best views, with Porto's old town tumbling down the Ribeira hills and **Vila Nova de Gaia**'s beautiful old warehouses on the far bank of the river. Gaia is home to Port lodges, upmarket hotels and restaurants, as well as more killer views of the city.

## /HOPPING

Independent shops dot Bombarda and the centre. Browse **Coração Alecrim** (Tavessa de Cedofeita 28), for its beautifully curated mix of vintage pieces and well-priced locally crafted leather work and homewares (they also have a beautiful 'real food' instore cafe). **Earlymade** (Rua do Rosário 235) and **Scar ID** (Rua do Rosário 253) both feature Porto designed fashion. If you've got no time to browse, head to the Bombarda shopping centre, aka **CCB** (Rua de Miguel Bombarda 285), where you'll find another cluster of vintage and young designer shops. **Lobo Taste** (Largo São Domingos 20) is a local favourite, with contemporary maker pieces that often have a nostalgic twist.

**POCKET TIP**
Local makers sell their wares at Urban Market every second Saturday, and more often in July, at either the outdoor Praça das Cardosas or indoor Hard Club.

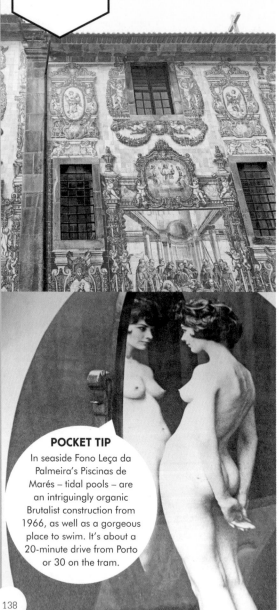

## ARCHITECTURE, ART & DE/IGN

Azulejos – blue ceramic tiles – have been part of the city's fabric since the 15th century and you can follow their blue haze all over town. **São Bento** train station's interior is covered in over 20,000 of them, the work depicting the founding of the Portuguese kingdom and its later empire. The **Igreja de Santo Ildefonso**'s astonishing elongated exterior dates to the 18th century, its azulejos' pious depictions are set against stern granite. Religious figures fill the exterior wall of the **Capela das Almas**, its blue expanse occupying a whole corner. Next to São Bento, look for the *Quem És, Porto?* mural, a contemporary, collaborative azulejo work created in 2014.

A new kind of wall decoration has also come to define Porto: street art. There are large murals in **Rua do Paraíso** and **Rua Miguel Bombarda**, at the **Trindade** train station, as well as in the **Miragaia** and **Vila Nova da Gaia** neighbourhoods. For indoor work, the **Fundação José Rodrigues** has a collection of the city's best street artists in a former factory.

The city's confidence is reflected in its contemporary architecture, which is plenty bold enough to divert your attention away from all the Baroque beauty, stately

**POCKET TIP**

In seaside Fono Leça da Palmeira's Piscinas de Marés – tidal pools – are an intriguingly organic Brutalist construction from 1966, as well as a gorgeous place to swim. It's about a 20-minute drive from Porto or 30 on the tram.

138

19th-century streetscapes and those miles of tiles. The asymmetrical forms of Rem Koolhaas' **Casa da Música** (Avenida da Boavista) are a taste, but you'll have to head a little out of the centre for the city's best. The **Museum of Contemporary Art at the Serralves Foundation** (Rua Dom João de Castro 210), designed by Álvaro Siza Vieira, one of the famed Porto School's leading figures, is a low-slung, almost ancient-feeling structure that crouches down into its green setting. It also happens to be one of the world's best contemporary art museums, with a huge collection of mostly post-1960 art and the country's most interesting temporary shows.

Design cred and art savvy can also be experienced at a more grassroots level. The **Design District**, centred around the **Rua Miguel Bombarda** and often referred to simply as **Bombarda**, gathers a number of commercial galleries, together with some artisan-led independent shops. **Presença** (no. 570), **Serpente** (no. 558), and **Quadrado Azul** (Rua Reinaldo Ferreira 20) show the country's best contemporary artists and have been around since the area's mid-1990s rebirth. They are joined by a current crop of spaces, including **Fernando Santos** (no. 526), **Aparte Galeria** (no. 221),

illustration gallery **O!** (no. 61) and artist-run space **Trindade** (no. 200). Simultaneous bimonthly openings across the district happen on Saturday afternoons.

## EATING & DRINKING

Whether you're hankering for simple Portuguese plates or an innovative dining experience, Porto's scene rarely disappoints.

Head to **Mercado Bolhão** (Rua Formosa) for stalls selling excellently prepared traditional dishes with amazing produce.

You'll be able to spot the best neighbourhood restaurants by their packed lunchtime tables, but one central one is the **Casa Viúva** (Rua Actor João Guedes 15) for no-fuss plates of chicken and chips, ribs or steaks.

Petiscos (Portuguese tapas) crawls are a great way to get to see the city if you're pressed for time. Begin yours at **RUA** (Travessa de Cedofeita 24), for pork cheek under walls graffitied by artist Mr. Dheo; get serious at **Caldeireiros** (Rua dos Caldeireiros 139), famed for their game sausages; then spend some time at the rustic communal table at **Brick Clérigos** (Campo dos Mártires da Pátria 103). Cross the river to try the seafood cataplana (an Algarve-style stir-fry) with grapes and saffron at slick **De Castro** (Avenida de Diogo Leite 162).

**POCKET TIP**

Forget sardines, Porto's favourite dish is the perfect big night out snack: the francesinha or frenchie, a groaning steak, sausage and ham sandwich smothered in melted gouda and spicy sauce.

**Oficina** (Rua de Miguel Bombarda 282) is the name for a car repair shop in Portugal and this stylish restaurant takes its name from the former mechanics' space that it now occupies. The chef is from the north-east and ingredients from this cool (as in climate) and wild region often feature on the contemporary menu.

**DOP** (Largo São Domingos 18) in the 14th-century Palácio das Artes, is another stylish option. That said, special occasion dining is made even more special on a rooftop with ocean breezes in Foz at simple, but spot-on, **Pedro Lemos** (Rua do Padre Luís Cabral 974).

For something simpler again, although deceptively, one of the city's most fashionable haunts is **Cafeína** (Rua do Padrão 100).

Porto grew rich on the profits of its wine trade and wine is still big business, none more so than the city's eponymous Port. Trying Port can be done in any wine bar, although tastings at one of the historic cellars or lodges in **Villa Nova de Gaia** is an atmospheric experience. **Cockburn's Lodge** (Rua Serpa Pinto 346) has one of the greatest collections of oak barrels and wooden vats of any Port cellar, while **W & J Graham's** (Rua Rei Ramiro) elegant cellars date back to 1890. Reservations required.

If Port is not your thing, the city is still a wonderful place to discover all else that the Douro Valley produces. **Wine Quay Bar** (Muro dos Bacalhoeiros 111) has an encyclopaedic list, as well as prime waterfront seating. For a good dose of Porto boho, **Maus Habitos** (Rua de Passos Manuel 17) hides itself in an apartment building and fluidly changes from bar, to club, to gallery, depending on the day and hour. Easier to find, **Café Candelabro** (Rua da Conceição 3) is an all day and night affair, with excellent wine, including interesting drops from the Azores, shoegaze tunes on the stereo and installation works in the window.

## SLEEPING

The sheer number of stylish little guesthouses tucked into historic buildings in this city is astonishing. These run across all budgets and are often comparably priced to Airbnbs. A handful of luxe, but not at all staid, hotels and good boutique hostels, make it a city where you'll be spoilt for choice, whether you choose to stay close to all in Ribiera, in the happening Bombarda or in one of the more upmarket districts, like Gaia, Boavista or Foz.

**Rosa et Al** (Rua do Rosário 233) epitomises the low-key style of the Design District

(Bombarda), with 1960s furniture, hand-crocheted throws, and its rooms have the high-ceiling proportions of its sprawling Belle Epoque townhouse home.

**Gallery Hostel** (Rua de Miguel Bombarda 222) gives you a similar cool, central location, historic bones and design savvy at bunk-bed prices.

A different look for Bombarda is the sleek, architectural lines of **Casa do Conto** (Rua da Boavista 703), its contemporary fit-out is intimate and full of nicely textured finishes.

In central, pedestrianised Rua das Flores, **Armazém Luxury Housing** (Largo São Domingos 74) has generously large rooms and nicely dramatic interiors that mix industrial finishes and luxe fabrics.

**M Maison Particulière**'s (Largo São Domingos 66) lush, classical aesthetics – stone walls, fireplaces and velvet furnishings – make it a great choice for a winter stay.

Also super central are the vintage-filled studio and one bed apartments of **Miss'opo** (Rua dos Caldeireiros 100), which also runs cultural projects in its book- and magazine-filled downstairs bar and cafe, and the design-filled and architecturally interesting **Bluesock Hostels** (Rua de São João 40).

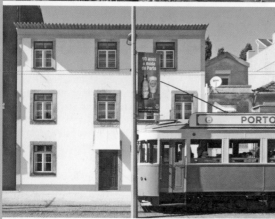

A short walk from the centre, up towards Mercado Bolhão and handy for the train station, **Malmerendas** (Rua Dr. Alves da Veiga 186) has super comfortable apartments in a lovely old house, a rare little garden and kind, personal service.

Staying in Foz can be a great way to combine a beach and city break – **Duas Portas** (Rua de Sobreiras 516) is just by the mouth of the Douro. Its minimalist fit-out is softened by the lovely human-scaled townhouse and its original touches, like raised ceilings and decorative wooden doors.

Upmarket urges are also well catered for in this carefree, stylish city. The little **1872 River House** (Rua do Infante D. Henrique 133) is, as the name suggests, right on the river and has eight rooms, decorated with a lovely attention to detail.

Across the Douro in Gaia, the **Yeatman** (Rua do Choupelo) is an indulgent pick for wine lovers, with a pool on the roof, and sexy, sexy rooms – in-room fireplaces, miles of marble, tinto-toned walls and, if you ask, circular beds.

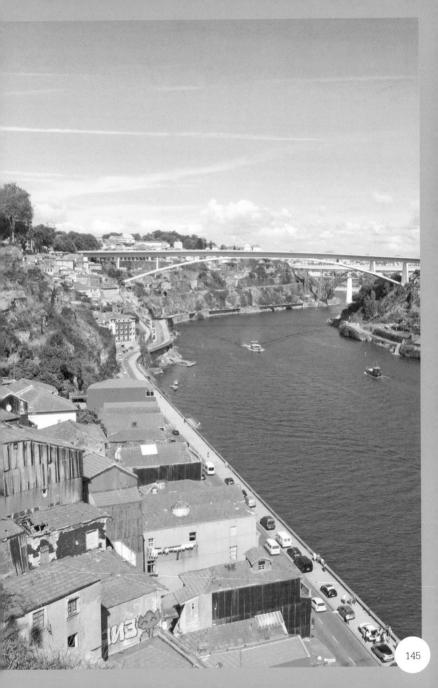

# TRAVEL TIPS

## GETTING TO LISBON

### Airport

The city's only airport is Aeroporto de Lisboa (aeroportolisboa.pt). It's a quick drive from the centre: 15 minutes outside of high peak hour. Taxis are plentiful but ensure the meter is turned on and you have an idea where you are going. Most locals recommend catching an **Uber** instead. They pick up in the Departures carpark, and at around €8 a trip, it's half of the cost of taxis.

There's a Metro (train) stop at the airport. Most downtown destinations like Baixa/Chiado and Cais do Sodré are on the green line, so change from the red line at Alameda. It's only around a 20-minute trip. The international train station Gare do Oriente is on the red line and around 10 minutes away. You'll need to buy a 7 Colinas/Viva Viagem travel card (see this page); it's €1.45 for a single trip.

The airport shuttle service can be easier if you have luggage, and it has wi-fi and USB chargers on board. **Aerobus** (aerobus.pt) departs from 7am to 11pm, from outside Arrivals (adult/child €3.60/2).

### Train

Lisbon's main train station is the Estação do Oriente, north-east of the city in the Parque das Nações district. The overnight service to Madrid, the Trenhotel Lusitania, departs from here, as well as from Santa Apolónia in Alfama.

All trains to Porto (see p. 134) depart from Santa Apolónia, while trains to Sintra (see p. 114) depart from Rossio and rail services to Cascais and Estoril leave from the Cais do Sodré station.

You can buy tickets to Porto or the south of Portugal from the **Portuguese Railways** website (www.cp.pt), with cheap advance-purchase fares available.

## GETTING AROUND LISBON

### Public transport

The main modes of public transport in Lisbon are: the Metro (train), buses, trams and funiculars. Ferries (see p. 107) also run across the Rio Tejo (River Tagus).

All can be accessed with a **7 Colinas/Viva Viagem** travel card. Buy cards at any train station. Cards cost €0.50 and can be loaded for single 'zapping' trips at €1.45 each. Day passes can also be loaded for €6.30. Unfortunately there are no weekly or monthly pass options for longer stays.

### Taxis & Ubers

Taxis and Ubers are cheap – it's hard to rack up much beyond €5 a trip in an Uber between any points in the city centre.

### Bike

Bike riding can be challenging in the steep, narrow streets of Lisbon, but there is a city-wide bike share system **Gira** (gira-bicicletasdelisboa.pt), and it has bike stations handy for the wonderful seven-kilometre (4.3 miles) bike path along the Rio Tejo (River Tagus).

## TIME ZONE

Lisbon Time is in Western European Standard Time (WET), which is Greenwich Mean Time (GMT). This is one hour behind the rest of Europe and the same as the UK. Portugal observes Summer Daylight-Saving Time.

## TOURIST INFORMATION

**Visit Lisboa** (visitlisboa.com), the city's tourist information organisation, has shopfront information hubs called **Ask Me Lisboa** at the airport, at Terreiro do Paço and Palácio Foz, near Avenida da Liberdade (see p. 61). The website has listings for sights and hotels, as well as a 'what's on page' for major events.

**Time Out** has a huge presence in the city and **Atlas Lisboa** has a useful events calendar (atlaslisboa.com/culture/events) for nightlife and alternative goings on.

## MONEY & ATMS

It's a good idea to have cash handy for coffee, drinks and for cheaper, casual restaurants, as EFTPOS is not as available as it is in some other European capitals.

Plan ahead on weekends as cash machines/ATMs in the main tourist zones have been known to run out of cash by Sunday afternoon and over long weekends.

## CLIMATE

Happy fact: Lisbon enjoys more daylight hours than any other capital in Europe. Officially Lisbon has a warm–temperate subtropical climate. That means its summers are hot and long and its winters are short and mild, though the city and coast are often drenched in the Atlantic's storms. Spring and autumn have many sunny days and these make for more pleasant exploring if you're visiting for the sights – the city's hilly terrain is sweaty work in high summer.

A surprise for many beach-loving visitors is the water temperature: it has a brief peak in late August at around 20°C (68 °F), but for the rest of the year, it's decidedly chilly.

## OPENING HOURS

Traditional shopping hours are from 9am or 10am–7pm, Monday to Friday, though many shops open over the weekend with reduced hours. Restaurants have lunch and dinner services but are less likely to turn away hungry diners in between these times than in other European countries. Evening service usually goes until 11pm or later.

Banks are open 8.30am–3pm, Monday to Friday.

Bars are open until 2am in the more residential neighbourhoods, Bairro Alto and Cais do Sodré around 3am, while those on the riverfront are open until 4am or later.

## USEFUL WORDS & PHRASES

Also see pp. 148–9 for ordering food, coffee and wine.

**Bom dia** Good morning
**Boa tarde** Good afternoon
**Boa noite** Good night
**Olá** Hi
**Obrigado/a** Thank you
**You're welcome** De nada/por nada
**Fala inglês?** Do you speak English?
**Tudo bem?** How are you?
**Onde você está?** Where are you?
**Gostaria de uma bica** I'd like an espresso
**Desculpe** Sorry
**Até breve!** See you later!

## SAFETY

Lisboetas are generally kind and helpful and the crime rate is low. Opportunistic crime however is not uncommon. Tourists are targeted by pickpockets on trams and you should be extra aware of your belongings around the Cais do Sodré, Anjos, Martim Moniz and Intendente Metro stations, especially at night.

Portugal famously decriminalised all drugs in 2001 but the persistent offers of pot, hash and cocaine from street dealers in areas like Bairro Alto should be ignored as possession is still illegal (the goods are often fake in any case).

## EATING & DRINKING

Lisbon's culinary life is one of tradition, innovation, comfort and surprise.

The city's restaurant scene is booming, with a vibrant, internationally acclaimed fine dining scene known for its youthful energy, sense of experimentation and broad roaming influences often drawn from Portugal's former colonies.

At the other end, the tasca and taberna, traditional eating places, have as strong a presence as ever. Never more crowded and local as at lunch, when everyone gathers for simple, wholesome traditional dishes, a jug of wine or a little glass of Sagres, these are the heart and soul of the city.

In between, there's an equally booming scene of casual dining reinterpretations of traditional dishes, a healthy crop of international cafes serving global brunch favourites and coffee, and many a reinvented street food place.

Lisbon also has, care of Portugal's ex-colonies, one of the world's most diverse culinary mixes, with fantastic Moçambiquan and Angolan restaurants, Goan places and Asian food care of Macau. Sushi, with the country's amazing fish and seafood supplies, is also hugely popular and reliably good.

Hard to find overseas and with a long and befuddling list of varietals due to its isolation over much of the 20th century, Portuguese wine is a wonderful discovery for wine lovers. A new generation of wine makers has seen an exponential increase in quality in the last decade or so, but often excellent wines are still cheap, even by European standards. If you're wanting to explore the scene, look for 'DOC' (Denominação de Origem Controlada) or 'DOP' (Denominação de Origem Protegida; the new pan-European denomination) wines, or vinho regionals (IGP), with less restrictions but still deeply regional. For everyday drinking or a long night out, table wines go by the simplest of names: vinho, that is wine.

### Ordering food

**Petiscos** small plate dining, such as: clams in garlic, salade de polvo (octopus salad), pastéis de bacalhau (cod fritters) and pica-pau (meat with pickles)

**Ovos mexidos** scrambled eggs, often served with sausage, bacalhau or seafood

**Peixinhos da horta** fried green beans

**Caldo verde** Soup made from potatoes, onions and bitter greens

**Feijoada** rustic bean stew, often cooked with pork or other meat

**Sardinhas assadas** grilled sardines, always served whole

**Polvo à lagareiro** tenderised, baked octopus with smashed potatoes

**Bacalhau à bras** shredded saltcod with eggs, olives and parsley

**Percebes** gooseneck barnacles, usually served in their gnarly shells

**Prego** garlic-studded minute steak in a crusty roll

**Bifana** sautéed strips of pork in a crusty roll

**Bitoque** steak served with a fried egg, rice, fried potatoes and salad

**Alheira** smoky, tangy sausage, made from game or chicken and bread

**Presunto** Portugal's version of prosciutto or jamón

**Leitão** roast suckling pig

**Queijo de Azeitão** a certified cheese made close to Lisbon, with a buttery centre

**Pastel de nata (plural pastéis) or pastel de Belém** Portuguese custard tart originating in Belém

**Bolo de Arroz** plain rice flour cupcake, a similar texture to the French madeleine

**Ginjinha, ginja** Lisbon's own liqueur, infused with ginja (sour cherry)

**Sagres, Super Bock** common tap beers, usually served as 'uma imperial' or 'uma cerveja', a 300ml glass

### Ordering coffee

**Uma bica** espresso

**Um pingo/pingado** cortado, piccolo

**Um garoto** a slightly larger cortado, similar to a three-quarter latte

**Meia de leite** foamy flat white-style (ask for escura if you want it stronger)

**Um galão** café latte, but usually milkier

**Um abatanado** long black

## Wine glossary

**Vinho tinto** red wine

**Vinho branco** white wine

**Port** fortified wine, made with port grapes

**Vinho verde** literally green wine, a fresh, young white from the north

**Espumante** simple sparkling wines, best from Távora-Varosa

### Wine regions

| | |
|---|---|
| Alentejo | Dão |
| Lisboa | Douro & Porto |
| Tejo | Minho |
| Setúbal | Madeira |
| Bairrada | Pico Island (Azores) |
| Beira Interior | Algarve |

### Wine varietals

**Trincadeira & Alicante Bouschet** fruity reds from the Alentejo

**Touriga Nacional** rich inky red from the Douro

**Arragônes & Tinta Roriz** Tempranillo from the Dão

**Alvarinho** floral and aromatic white from the Minho

**Fernão Pires** young, floral and fruity white from Lisboa and Tejo

**Arinto & Pedernã** lemony, mineral white from Lisboa's Bucelas

**Encruzado** fine, full-bodied white from the Dão

## TIPPING

Tipping is not obligatory but ten per cent for good service is welcome and a nice gesture in a country where wages are low.

## MUSIC

Fado is Portugal's national cultural treasure and Lisbon is its home. In addition to the melancholy vocals and distinctive guitar of this compelling art form, the city's complex colonial history has endowed the city with an incredibly rich and constantly evolving contemporary musical scene.

Kuduro, kizomba, funaná and tarraxinha are all genres that emerged from Angola, Mozambique, Cabo Verde, São Tomé and Príncipe, while all of Brazil's multifarious musical styles are well represented, too. These come together in various forms, such as batida, Afro-house and other Afro-electronic styles and further Latin-tinged Lusophone hybrids.

Music label **Discos Principe** (principediscos.bandcamp.com) is a great place to get acquainted with Lisbon's unique sound, while word-of-mouth (really, just ask) and social media will lead you to various club nights around town.

## LGBTQIA+

Lisbon's scene is a lively one. Look to **Lisbon Gay Circuit** (lisbongaycircuit.com) for listings of clubs, bars, parties, saunas and community events.

Reliable mixed venues include **LuxFrágil** (*see* p. 23), while gay bars and clubs can be found in Príncipe Real and the 'gay corner' of Rua da Baroca and Tavessa da Espera in Bairro Alto. Costa Caparica's (*see* p. 104) southern strip has a number of gay-friendly nude beaches, such as Praia 19, Meco and Praia da NATO/Adiça.

**Lisboa Pride** (lisboapride.com) is held in June.

## PUBLIC HOLIDAYƧ

Beyond banks and government offices, holiday observance is not exactly consistent, with many bars, shops and restaurants remaining open.

**Ano Novo (New Year's Day)** 1 January

**Carnaval** February/March, the Tuesday before Ash Wednesday

**Sexta-feira Santa (Good Friday)** March/April

**Dia da Liberdade (Liberty Day)** 25 April

**Dia do Trabalhador (Labour Day)** 1 May

**Corpo de Deus (Corpus Christi)** May/June (ninth Thursday after Easter)

**Dia de Portugal, de Camões e das Comunidades Portuguesas (Portugal Day, aka Camões)** 10 June

**Dia de Santo António (Feast of St Anthony, Lisbon's municipal holiday)** 13 June

**Assunção (Assumption)** 15 August

**Implantação da República (Republic Day)** 5 October

**Dia de Todos-os-Santos (All Saints' Day)** 1 November

**Independência (Independence Day)** 1 December

**Imaculada Conceição (Feast of the Immaculate Conception)** 8 December

**Natal (Christmas Day)** 25 December

## FEƧTIVALƧ

See the What's On section of **Visit Lisboa** (visitlisboa.com) tourist website for details of festivals.

The traditional Festas dos Santos Populares (Popular Saints Parties) takes over the city from early June, when much of the historic centre, especially streets like Rua Guia in Mouraria and Rua dos Remédios in Alfama drip with colourful garlands and fairy lights. The most spectacular of these is the Dia de Santo António, dedicated to the city's favourite saint, beginning on the evening of 12 June. The next night, the street parades, the Marchas Populares, take place on Avenida da Liberdade: hundreds of singers and dancers from each of the city's different traditional neighbourhoods compete in front of huge crowds. Join Lisboeta during the festivities for a city-wide feast of sweet seasonal sardines or pork belly and ribs, grilled over coals on what seems like every street corner. Fireworks also light up the Tejo, once the performances on Avenida da Liberdade are over. Cheap beer and sangria and a soundtrack of pimba – Portugal's dancey, double entendre-filled alternative to fado music – keep the party going late into the night.

During the festival period look out for stalls selling pots of basil, (manjerico in Portuguese) given as a symbol of affection, as well as a selection of poems and paper carnations.

## ƧURFING

Portugal is Europe's most swell-blessed nation and good breaks can be found less than 30 minutes from the centre of Lisbon. The closest are at Carcavelos, accessible by train from Cais do Sodré. Costa Caparica (*see* p. 104), across the Ponte 25 de Abril (25 April Bridge), also has kilometres of beaches and a handful of well-known breaks. Both beaches have surf hire shops or try **BOUTIK** (*see* p. 52) in the city's São Bento.

## PHONE & WI-FI

Portugal's country code is +351, Lisbon city's is 21.

Most cafes, bars and restaurants have free wi-fi, though you'll often have to ask for the password.

**MEO** (meo.pt) has traveller-friendly voice and data, or data-only SIM deals. There's a handy branch in the very central Armazéns do Chiado mall. Staff are super helpful and waits are usually minimal.

Other operators include: **NOS**, **Orange** and **Vodafone**, the latter is said to have better coverage throughout the country, if you're travelling beyond the cities.

## EMBASSIES & CONSULATES

### Australia
Avenida da Liberdade 200
portugal.embassy.gov.au
21 310 1500
Mon–Fri 10am–4pm

### Britain
Rua de São Bernardo 33
www.gov.uk/contact-consulate-lisbon
21 392 40 00
Mon–Fri 9am–1pm & 2.30–5pm

### USA
Avenida das Forças Armadas 133C
pt.usembassy.gov
21 727 3300
Mon–Fri 8am–5pm

### Canada
Avenida da Liberdade 196
canadainternational.gc.ca/portugal
21 316 4600
Mon–Fri 9am–12pm

## ACCOMMODATION

There are a huge number of hotels, hostels, guesthouses and short-term rentals throughout the city. While soulless Airbnbs have started to characterise the scene, keep looking, and look a little out of the centre, and you can still find beautifully authentic and charming apartments. Note that prices do rise steeply in summer and can also spike on weekends from April to October.

### Best budget hotels
The Independente Hostel & Suites (theindependente.pt)
Home Lisbon Hostel (homelisbonhostel.com)

### Best midrange hotels
The Lisboans (thelisboans.com)
The Vintage Hotel & Spa (thevintagelisbon.com)
1908 Hotel (1908lisboahotel.com)

### Best luxury hotels
Palacio Belmonte (palaciobelmonte.com)
Santa Clara 1728 (silentliving.pt)

1

B

C

AMADORA

BENFICA

2

OEIRAS

AJUDA

BELÉM

LISBON

TO CASCAIS
PG 172

170–1

3

Tejo

Rio

4

A

B

C

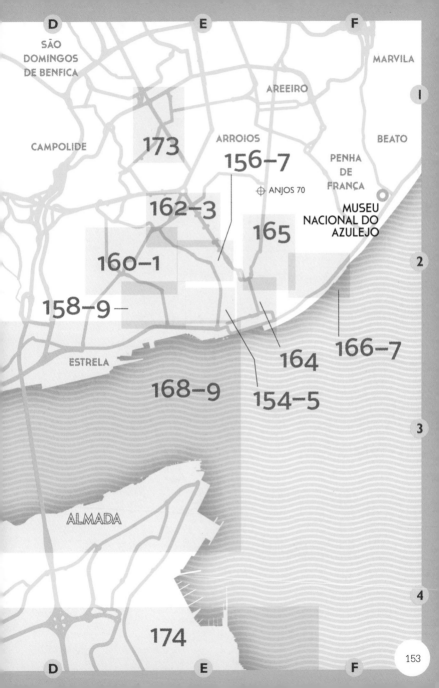

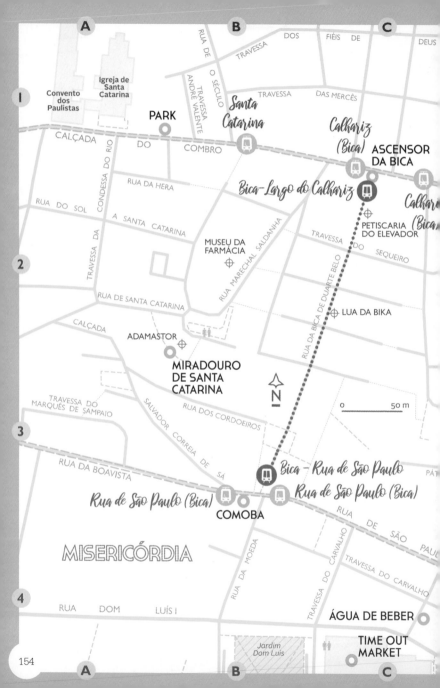

**D**
TASCA DO CHICO
É DOS OIS & 9 DA ZDB
TRAVESSA DA ESPERA

**E**
Espaço Chiado (shopping centre)

RUA DA TRINDADE

**F**
TRAVESSA DO CARMO

**I**

SANTA MARIA MAIOR

RUA DAS GÁVEAS

JA DAS SALGADEIRAS

**MANTEIGARIA**

*Praça Luís de Camões*

RUA NOVA DA TRINDADE

CAFÉ A BRASILEIRA

RUA GARRETT

Cinema Ideal

*Praça Luís de Camões*

PARIS EM LISBOA

*Chiado*

**LIVRARIA BERTRAND**

A DA HORTA SÊCA

RUA SERPA

RUA ANCHIETA

A VIDA PORTUGUESA

**2**

**A TABERNA DA RUA DAS FLORES**

*Chiado*

LARGO

PLUS351

RUA DA EMENDA

**PALACIO CHIADO**

RUA PINTO

RUA CAPELO

**FÁBRICA COFFEE ROASTERS**

TRAVESSA DE GUILHERME COSSOUL

DO PICADEIRO

Teatro Nacional de São Carlos

MUSEU NACIONAL DE ARTE CONTEMPORÂNEA DO CHIADO (MNAC)

RUA SERPA PINTO

**3**

RUA DAS FLORES

RUA ANTÓNIO MARIA CARDOSO

RUA DO ALECRIM

**BY THE WINE**

São Luiz Teatro Municipal

PIMENTA

DO

RUA DAS FLORES

MUSEU NACIONAL DE ARTE CONTEMPORÂNEA DO CHIADO (MNAC)

*Rua Vítor Cordon / Rua Serpa Pinto*

**4**

*Rua de São Paulo*

*Rua Vítor Cordon*

RUA VICTOR CORDON

O BOM O MAU E O VILÃO

*Rua do Alecrim*

PENSÃO AMOR

BACCHANAL

RUA DO FERRAGIAL

LARGO DO CORPO SANTO

*Corpo Santo*

**D**

**E**

**F**

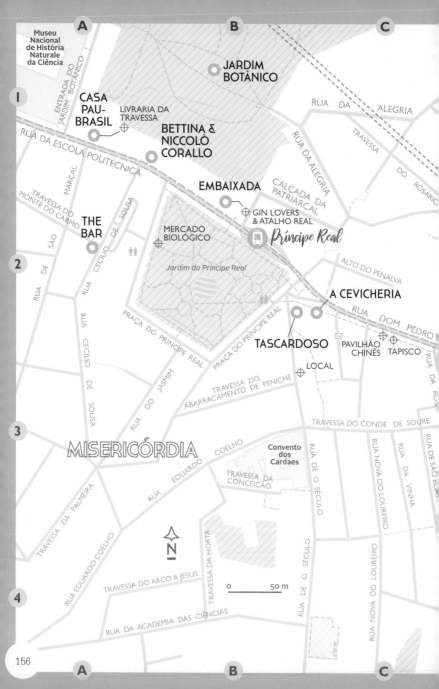

Museu Nacional de História Naturale da Ciência

JARDIM BOTÂNICO

CASA PAU-BRASIL

LIVRARIA DA TRAVESSA

BETTINA & NICCOLÒ CORALLO

RUA DA ESCOLA POLITÉCNICA

EMBAIXADA

CALÇADA DA PATRIARCAL

RUA DA ALEGRIA

RUA DA ALEGRIA

TRAVESSA

DO ROSÁRIO

GIN LOVERS & ATALHO REAL

Príncipe Real

THE BAR

MERCADO BIOLÓGICO

Jardim do Príncipe Real

ALTO DO PENALVA

A CEVICHERIA

RUA DOM PEDRO

TASCARDOSO

PAVILHÃO CHINÊS

TAPISCO

LOCAL

PRAÇA DO PRÍNCIPE REAL

PRAÇA DO PRÍNCIPE REAL

TRAVESSA DO ABARRACAMENTO DE PENICHE

TRAVESSA DO CONDE DE SOURE

MISERICÓRDIA

Convento dos Cardaes

TRAVESSA DA CONCEIÇÃO

RUA EDUARDO COELHO

RUA DE O SÉCULO

RUA NOVA DO LOUREIRO

RUA DA VINHA

RUA DE SÃO BO

TRAVESSA DA PALMEIRA

RUA EDUARDO COELHO

TRAVESSA DA HORTA

RUA DE O SÉCULO

RUA NOVA DO LOUREIRO

N

0    50 m

TRAVESSA DO ARCO A JESUS

RUA DA ACADEMIA DAS CIÊNCIAS

TRAVESSA DO MONTE DO CARMO

RUA MARÇAL

RUA DE SÃO

RUA CECÍLIO DE SOUSA

RUA CECÍLIO DE SOUSA

RUA CECÍLIO DE SOUSA

RUA DO JASMIM

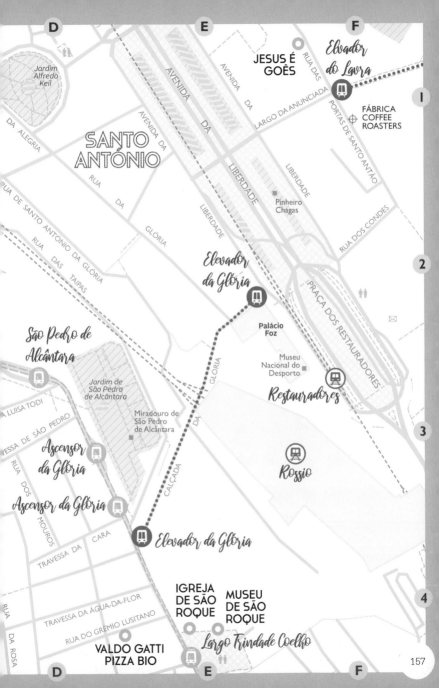

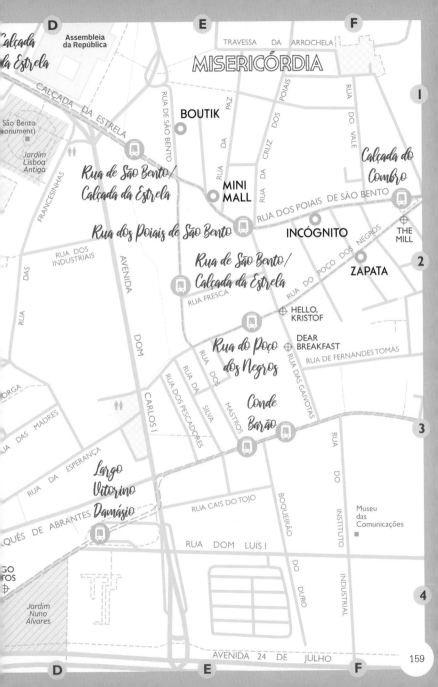

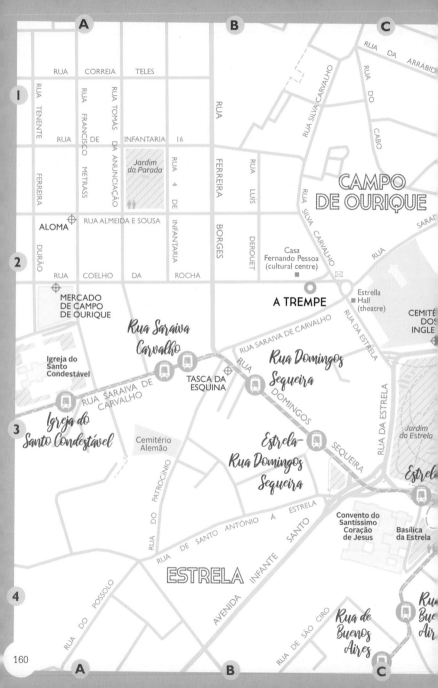

A

B

C

1

2

3

4

RUA CORREIA TELES

RUA TENENTE

RUA FRANCISCO DE

RUA TOMÁS DA ANUNCIAÇÃO

FERREIRA

METRASS

INFANTARIA 16

Jardim da Parada

RUA 4 DE

RUA SILVA CARVALHO

RUA DA ARRÁBID

RUA DO CABO

CAMPO DE OURIQUE

ALOMA

RUA ALMEIDA E SOUSA

INFANTARIA

RUA FERREIRA BORGES

RUA LUÍS

DERQUET

RUA SILVA CARVALHO

RUA SARA

DURÃO

RUA COELHO DA ROCHA

Casa Fernando Pessoa (cultural centre)

A TREMPE

Estrella Hall (theatre)

CEMITÉ DOS INGLE

MERCADO DE CAMPO DE OURIQUE

Rua Saraiva Carvalho

RUA SARAIVA DE CARVALHO

Rua Domingos Sequeira

RUA DA ESTRELA

Igreja do Santo Condestável

RUA SARAIVA DE CARVALHO

TASCA DA ESQUINA

RUA DOMINGOS

Igreja do Santo Condestável

Cemitério Alemão

Estrela- Rua Domingos Sequeira

SEQUEIRA

RUA DA ESTRELA

Jardim da Estrela

Estrel

RUA DO PATROCÍNIO

RUA DE SANTO ANTÓNIO À ESTRELA

SANTO

Convento do Santíssimo Coração de Jesus

Basílica da Estrela

ESTRELA

AVENIDA INFANTE SANTO

RUA DO POSSOLO

RUA DE SÃO CIRO

Rua de Buenos Aires

Rua Bue Air

A

B

C

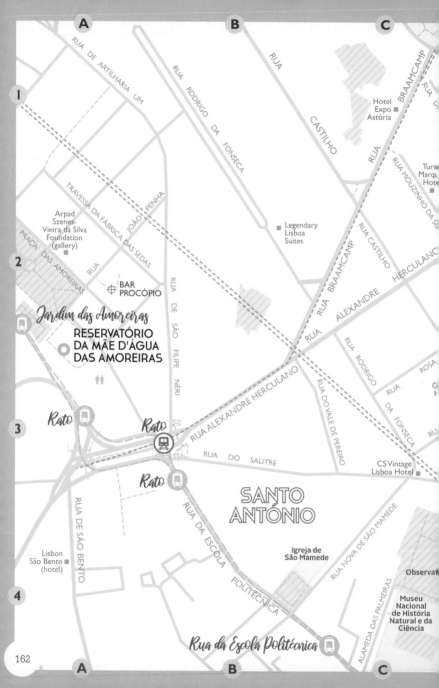

# D

RUA RODRIGUES SAMPAIO

AVENIDA DA LIBERDADE

m Av
rdade
Hotel

## ASSOCIAÇÃO CABOVERDEANA

## DELIDELUX

Hotel
Porto Bay
Liberdade

Hotel
Vincii

ARAUJO

Casa-Museu
Medeiros
e Almeida

SALGUEIRO

Hotel
orge V

Cinemateca
Portuguesa-
Museu do
Cinema

CASTILHO

RATA

# E

RUA ALEXANDRE HERCULANO

RUA RODRIGUES SAMPAIO

RUA DE SANTA MARTA

N

TRAVESSA DE SANTA MARTA

OPEN
BRASSERIE
MEDITERRÂNICA

RUA DO PRIOR COUTINHO

TRAVESSA DAS PARREIRAS

RUA BARATA SALGUEIRO

AVENIDA DA LIBERDADE

RUA RODRIGUES SAMPAIO

RUA DE SANTA MARTA

TRAVESSA DO LOUREIRO

Hotel
Lisboa

Hotel
Britania

# F

RUA DE SANTA MARTA

0          100 m

RUA DO PASSADICO

RUA DO CARDAL DE SÃO JOSÉ

I

2

Tivoli
Lisboa
Hotel

## SKY BAR

AVENIDA DA LIBERDADE

AVENIDA DA LIBERDADE

## JNCQUOI

ASSOULINE

FASHION
CLINIC

3

Avani
Avenida
Liberdade
(hotel)

*Avenida* 🚇

RUA DO SALITRE

AVENIDA DA

AVENIDA DA LIBERDADE

Valverde
Hotel

Fontecruz
Lisboa
(hotel)

## JARDIM BOTÂNICO

## AVENIDA DA LIBERDADE ARCHITECTURE

Cineteatro
Capitólio-
Teatro Raúl
Solnado

Sofitel
Lisbon
Liberdade

LIBERDADE

4

*Jardim
Alfredo
Keil*

# D

# E

# F

**ARROIOS**

A VIDA PORTUGUESA

CASA INDEPENDENTE

HOTEL 1908

CERVEJARIA RAMIRO

RUA NOVA DO DESTERRO

JOSEPHINE

RUA DE SÃO LÁZARO

RUA DA PALMA

RUA DA PALMA

Rua da Palma

RUA DA PALMA

RUA DO BENFORMOSO

ARQUIVO FOTOGRÁFICO DE LISBOA

0          100 m

N

TOPO

Martim Moniz

Socorro

RUA DA PALMA

OS AMIGOS DA SEVERA

RUA DOS CAVALEIROS

Praça Dom Duarte

TRAM 28E

CHINÊS CLANDESTINO

ESCADINHAS DA SAÚDE

RUA

Martim Montiz

Hospital de Bonecas The Doll Hospital-museum

My Story Hotel Tejo

ZÉ DOS CORNOS

Rossio

CANTINHO DO AZIZ

RUA MARQUÊS DE PONTE DE LIMA

COSTA DO CASTELO

SANTA MARIA MAIOR

CASTELO DE SÃO JORGE

Praça da Figueira

RUA DA PRATA

Viewpoint

Viewpoint

Viewpoint

GRENACHE & PALÁCIO BELMONTE

Sapadores

MONTEIRO

SÃO VICENTE

RUA DAMASCENO

BOMBARDA

RUA DA SENHORA DO MONTE

Rua da Graça

VINO VERO

CALÇADA DA SENHORA DO MONTE

RUA DAMASCENO MONTEIRO

RUA DAS OLARIAS

RUA DOS LAGARES

Jardim da Cerca da Graça

Graça

Convento da Graça

Igreja da Graça

Jardim Augusto Gil

Largo do Terreirinho

MIRADOURO DA GRAÇA

Rua dos Lagares

São Tomé

Largo das Portas do Sol

DAMAS

TRAVESSA DE SÃO VICENTE

FEIRA DA LADRA

RUA DA VERÓ

CEIA ⊕

RUA DE SANTA CLARA

Mercado de Santa Clara

TRAVESSA DAS MÓNICAS

Voz do Operário

ARCO GRANDE DE CIMA

CAMPO

RUA DA VOZ DO OPERÁRIO

Largo de São Vicente

RUA DE SÃO VICENTE

Igreja de São Vicente de Fora

N

0 ——————— 100 m

CALÇADA DE SÃO VICENTE

Calçada de São Vicente

TASCA BELA ⊕

Rua das Escolas Gerais

RUA DAS

RUA DOS CORVOS

ESCOLAS

GERAIS

GUILHERME

BRAGA

RUA

DO VIGÁRIO ⊕

RUA DO VIGÁRIO

Largo das Portas do Sol

FADO NA MORGADINHA

BAR TEJO ○

AGULHA NO PALHEIRO

Miradouro de Santo Estêvão

RUA DE SANTO ESTÊVÃO

RUA DA REGUEIRA

DOS REMÉDIOS

JARDIM DO TABACO

⊕ MIRADOURO DE SANTA LUZIA

RUA DE SÃO MIGUEL

DO

SANTA MARIA MAIOR

RUA DOS

RUA DO

RUA DO TERREIRO DO TRIGO

Largo do Chafariz de Dentro

AVENIDA INFANTE DON

Largo de São Miguel

⊕ MUSEU DO FADO

166

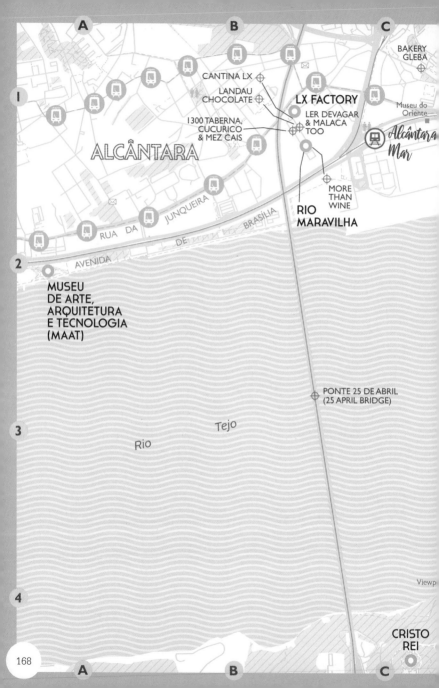

A

B

C

1

BAKERY GLEBA

CANTINA LX

LANDAU CHOCOLATE

LX FACTORY

LER DEVAGAR & MALACA TOO

Museu do Oriente

1300 TABERNA, CUCURICO & MEZ CAIS

ALCÂNTARA

Alcântara Mar

MORE THAN WINE

JUNQUEIRA

RIO MARAVILHA

RUA DA

DE

BRASILIA

2

AVENIDA

MUSEU DE ARTE, ARQUITETURA E TECNOLOGIA (MAAT)

Rio

Tejo

3

PONTE 25 DE ABRIL (25 APRIL BRIDGE)

4

Viewp

CRISTO REI

168

A

B

C

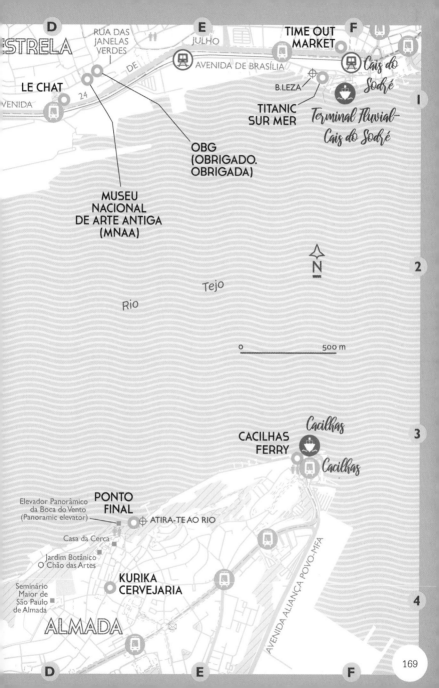

Calçada da Ajuda (GNR)

Rua de Dom Vasco

Rua da Bica do Marquês

Boa Hora

ADJUDA

Jardim Botânico d'Ajuda

GONÇALVES ZARCO

RUA

CALÇADA DO GALVÃO

AJUDA

CALÇADA DA

0      200 m

RUA ALEXANDRE DE SÁ PINTO

N

2

CALÇADA DO GALVÃO

Jardim Botânico Tropical

CALÇADA DO GALVÃO

TABERNA DOS FERREIROS

PASTÉIS DE BELÉM

CALÇADA DA AJUDA

Palácio Nacional de Belém

Altinho (MAAT)

Belém

RUA DA JUNQUEIRA

STEIRO OS ONIMOS

RUA DOS JERÓNIMOS

Mosteiro dos Jerónimos

Jardim Vasco da Gama

Jardim Afonso de Albuquerque

Museu Nacional dos Coches

Belém

Belém

MUSEU DE ARTE, ARQUITETURA E TECNOLOGIA (MAAT)

Praça Império

AVENIDA DA ÍNDIA

Rosa dos Ventos

Doca de Belém

BELEM-PORTO BRANDÃO FERRY

Belém

PADRÃO DOS DESCOBRIMENTOS (MONUMENT)

Rio      Tejo

3

4

A B C

I

RUA JOAQUIM EIREIRA

AVENIDA ENGENHEIRO ADELINO AMARO DA COSTA

RUA DE SÃO JOSÉ

RUA DE ALVIDE

Jardim Tenente Álvaro Machado

N

Parque da Pereira

Parque do Ringue

RUA DA TORRE

Parque da Torre

AVENIDA INFANTE DOM HENRIQUE

CASCAIS

AVENIDA DE SINTRA

Cemitério Municipal da Guia

Parque Urbano da Ribeira dos mochos

RUA DE ABRIL

Grutas do Poço Velho (underground tunnel & cave)

2

Cascais

Pestana Cascais Ocean & Conference Aparthotel

25 DE ABRIL

Museu do Mar Rei Dom Carlos

O CANTINHO DA BELINHA

LARGO DA PRA DA RAIN

CASA DA GUIA

AVENIDA DA REPÚBLICA

AVENIDA

Jardins do Museu do Mar

Jardim da Parada

Palácio da Cidadela de Cascais

Parque Natural de Sintra-Cascais

CASA DAS HISTORIAS PAULA REGO

Parque Marechal Carmona

Marin de Casca

Boca do Inferno (natural rock arch)

Grande Real Villa Italia Hotel

Museu Condes de Castro Guimarães

3

Atlantic Ocean

4

172

A B C

0 500 m

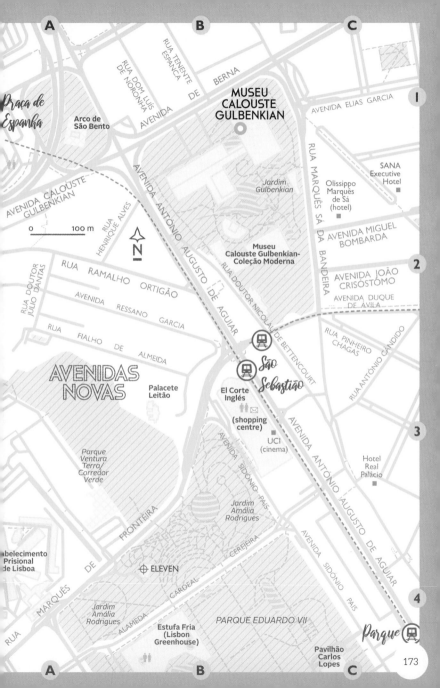

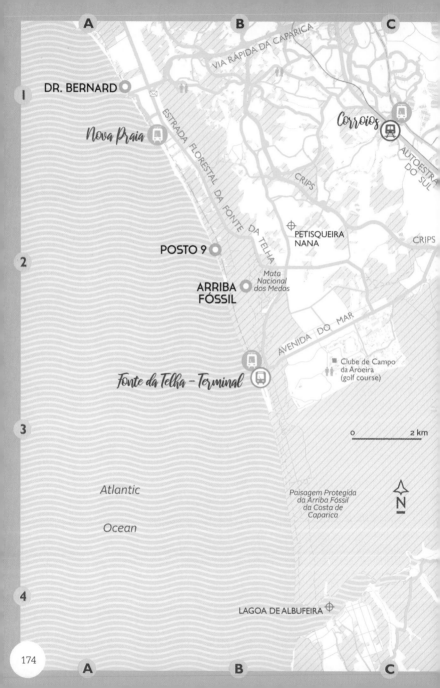

DR. BERNARD

Nova Praia

ESTRADA FLORESTAL DA FONTE DA TELHA

VIA RÁPIDA DA CAPARICA

Corroios

CRIPS

AUTOESTRADA DO SUL

PETISQUEIRA NANA

CRIPS

POSTO 9

ARRIBA FÓSSIL

Mata Nacional dos Medos

AVENIDA DO MAR

Clube de Campo da Aroeira (golf course)

Fonte da Telha – Terminal

Atlantic

Ocean

0        2 km

Paisagem Protegida da Arriba Fóssil da Costa de Caparica

N

LAGOA DE ALBUFEIRA

A            B            C

# INDEX

## ABOUT THE AUTHOR

Lisbon's maritime history, postcolonial cultural mix and progressive politics drew me in many years ago and has continued to fascinate. I returned recently to witness a city in the throes of rapid transformation; this latest research trip allowed me to explore that 'new' Lisbon in exquisite depth, as well as really reacquaint myself with the vibrant, multilayered city, and the food, wine, music and architecture, that I have always loved. This book comes after writing on Paris for Hardie Grant's Precincts and Pocket Precincts series, as well as twelve years writing guidebooks and features on Italy, France, North Africa, Belgium, Austria and Norway for Lonely Planet. I'm also a DK Travel author and have written on contemporary art, architecture and design for various international publishers and I am a frequent contributor to the *Telegraph* UK's travel section. Sydney born and bred, Melbourne domiciled for a few decades, I divide my time between Sydney, Paris' 11th, an imaginary masseria in Puglia and whichever other destination has currently cast its spell on me.

## ACKNOWLEDGEMENT/

The Lisboeta are some of the warmest and most welcoming people I've ever met and I have enormous gratitude for the kindness and care I received during this research trip. Big thanks go to Nicholas Wrathall and Daniel Nettheim for taking the 4am finishes in your strides. To Eugenie Kawabata for Lisbon wanderings and for sharing your adventures, likewise to Elizabeth Tremblay for great company and tips. Thanks to Teresa Ruiz for the warmest welcome and many fabulous leads, and to Gregory Bernard for the sunniest Caparica days, a crazy Lisbon night and Paris fun. To Luke Davies, for again conjuring the spirit and the storm, sweet Rome respite and LA languor. Thanks to Simon Duran Cordova for Caparica insights and images. Much gratitude to Teresa Barros and Margot Rident for Comporta intelligence and hospitality, to Chris Kraus at Outpost Arribas for a warm welcome and great local knowledge, and to Sofia d'Aguiar and Tomás Colaço for sharing your extraordinary home. As ever, much gratitude to Joe Guario for the tunes, the road, the coffee. Bises to Justin Westover in Paris for sorting my keys in the unholy hours after an emergency mid-flight turn-back. Back in Melbourne, thanks to Alice Barker, Melissa Kayser and Jessica Smith at Hardie Grant.

## PHOTO CREDIT/

All images are © Donna Wheeler, except the following:

Page iv, vi bottom left & 34 Natalia Horinkova; 2 middle, 38, 41 top, 95, 106–107 Bigstock; 23 André Dinis Carrilho; 56 middle Albedo; 57 bottom Sourced; 59 & 61 bottom William J. Sisti; 62–63 Delidelux; 65 Associação Caboverdeana; 66 Tivoli Hotels; 93 & 177 bottom Paulo Silva; 96 bottom & 97 top Luísa Ferreira, artworks © Paula Rego; 99 Darwin's Café; 101 & 178 lower middle Pastéis de Belém; 103 O Cantinho da Belinha; 108 top Isa; 109 Susanne Nilsson; 113 Simon Duran Cordova & Posto 9; 115–116, 117 top & 118 Posto de Turismo de Sintra; 120 top Chris Kraus, bottom Nortada; 121 Bar do Fondo; 122 top Lawrence's, bottom Casal de Santa Maria; 132 top, 133 middle & bottom Mateus Aires; 132 bottom & 133 top Nelson Garrido; 139 top Serralves Foundation, middle Danica O. Kus, bottom António Amen; 140 top & bottom Jorge Franganillo; 141 top Ewan Munro;.142 top & 143 middle 1872 River House; 142 bottom, 143 top & bottom Carlos Trancoso & Mariana Lopes; 144 bottom Jackietraveller Porto/Alamy Stock Photo; 178 bottom Unsplash/Licor Beirao.

Published in 2020 by Hardie Grant Travel, a division of Hardie Grant Publishing

Hardie Grant Travel (Melbourne)
Building 1, 658 Church Street
Richmond, Victoria 3121

Hardie Grant Travel (Sydney)
Level 7, 45 Jones Street
Ultimo, NSW 2007

www.hardiegrant.com/au/travel

The maps in this publication incorporate data from:

© OpenStreetMap contributors
OpenStreetMap is made available under the Open Data Commons Open Database License (ODbL) by the OpenStreetMap Foundation (OSMF): http://opendatacommons.org/licenses/odbl/1.0/. Any rights in individual contents of the database are licensed under the Database Contents License: http://opendatacommons.org/licenses/dbcl/1.0/
Data extracts via Geofabrik GmbH https://www.geofabrik.de
© CM Lisboa 2019 – data made available under Creative Commons CCZero License

A catalogue record for this book is available from the National Library of Australia

Lisbon Pocket Precincts
ISBN 9781741176537

10 9 8 7 6 5 4 3 2 1

**Publisher**
Melissa Kayser

**Project editor**
Megan Cuthbert

**Editor**
Alice Barker

**Proofreader**
Jessica Smith

**Cartographer**
Emily Maffei

**Design**
Michelle Mackintosh

**Typesetting**
Megan Ellis

**Index**
Max McMaster

**Prepress**
Megan Ellis and
Splitting Image
Colour Studio

Printed in Singapore by 1010 Printing
International Limited

**Disclaimer:** While every care is taken to ensure the accuracy of the data within this product, the owners of the data do not make any representations or warranties about its accuracy, reliability, completeness or suitability for any particular purpose and, to the extent permitted by law, the owners of the data disclaim all responsibility and all liability (including without limitation, liability in negligence) for all expenses, losses, damages (including indirect or consequential damages) and costs which might be incurred as a result of the data being inaccurate or incomplete in any way and for any reason.

**Publisher's Disclaimers:** The publisher cannot accept responsibility for any errors or omissions. The representation on the maps of any road or track is not necessarily evidence of public right of way. The publisher cannot be held responsible for any injury, loss or damage incurred during travel. It is vital to research any proposed trip thoroughly and seek the advice of relevant state and travel organisations before you leave.

**Publisher's Note:** Every effort has been made to ensure that the information in this book is accurate at the time of going to press. The publisher welcomes information and suggestions for correction or improvement.

# POCKET PRECINCT/ /ERIE/

## COLLECT THE /ET!

The Pocket Precincts are curated guidebooks offering the best cultural, eating and drinking spots to experience the city as the locals do. Each guidebook includes detailed maps at the back and a field trip section encouraging you to venture further afield.

These compact guides are perfect for slipping into your back pocket before you head out on your next adventure.

## COMING /OON